# The Canons of Hippolytus:

## An English version, with introduction and annotation and an accompanying Arabic text

Alistair C. Stewart

SCD Press
2021

*The Canons of Hippolytus. An English version, with introduction and annotation and an accompanying Arabic Text*
(Early Christian Studies, 22)
By Alistair C. Stewart© 2021

SCD Press
PO Box 1882
Macquarie Centre NSW 2113
Australia
scdpress@scd.edu.au

All rights reserved. No part of this book may be reproduced or transmitted in any form or by any means, electronic or mechanical, including photocopying, recording or by any information and storage system without permission in writing from the publishers.

ISBN-13: 978-1-925730-25-8 (paperback)
ISBN-13: 978-1-925730-26-5 (ebook)

Layout and design by: Lankshear Design Pty Ltd
Printed and bound by: Ingram Spark

# The Canons of Hippolytus:

## An English version, with introduction and annotation and an accompanying Arabic text

Alistair C. Stewart

SCD Press
2021

# Early Christian Studies 22

## SCD Press Editorial Board

Professor Diane Speed

Professor James R. Harrison

Professor Peter G. Bolt

## Additional Series Editors

Professor Pauline Allen (Australian Catholic University)

Professor Wendy Mayer (Australian Lutheran College)

Professor Bronwen Neil (Macquarie University)

# Early Christian Studies

1. Jan Harm Barkhuizen, *Proclus Bishop of Constantinople. Homilies on the Life of Christ* (2001).
2. Robert C. Hill, *Theodoret of Cyrus. Commentary on the Song of Songs* (2001).
3. Johan Ferreira, *The Hymn of the Pearl* (2002).
4. Alistair Stewart-Sykes, *The Life of Polycarp. An anonymous vita from third-century Smyrna* (2002).
5. Daniel Van Slyke, *Quodvultdeus of Carthage. The Apocalyptic Theology of a Roman African in Exile* (2003).
6. Bronwen Neil & Pauline Allen, *The Life of Maximus the Confessor. Recension 3* (2003).
7. George Kalantzis, *Theodore of Mopsuestia. Commentary on the Gospel of John* (2004).
8. Rudolf Brändle, *John Chrysostom. Bishop – Reformer – Martyr* (2004).
9. J. Mark Armitage, *A Twofold Solidarity. Leo the Great's Theology of Redemption* (2005).
10. Alistair Stewart-Sykes, *The Apostolic Church Order. The Greek Text with Introduction, Translation and Annotation* (2006, 2021).
11. Geoffrey D. Dunn, *Cyprian and the Bishops of Rome: Questions of Papal Primacy in the Early Church* (2007, 2018).
12. Pauline Allen, Majella Franzmann, & Rick Strelan (eds.), *"I Sowed Fruits into Hearts" (Odes Sol. 17:13). Festschrift for Professor Michael Lattke* (2007).
13. David Luckensmeyer & Pauline Allen (eds.), *Studies of Religion and Politics in the Early Christian Centuries* (2010).
14. Oliver Herbel, *Sarapion of Thmuis: Against the Manicheans and Pastoral Letters* (2011).

15. Raymond Laird, *Mindset, Moral Choice and Sin in the Anthropology of John Chrysostom* (2012, 2017).
16. Alexander L. Abecina, *Time and Sacramentality in Gregory of Nyssa's Contra Eunomium* (2013).
17. Johan Ferreira, *Early Chinese Christianity: The Tang Christian Monument and Other Documents* (2014).
18. Wendy Mayer & Ian J. Elmer (eds.), *Men and Women in the Early Christian Centuries* (2014).
19. Silouan Fotineas, *The Letters of Bishop Basil of Caesarea: Instruments of Communion* (2018).
20. Andrey Romanov, *One God as One God and One Lord. The Lordship of Jesus Christ as a Hermeneutical Key to Paul's Christology in 1 Corinthians (with a special focus on 1 Cor 8:6)* (2021).
21. Hyueng Guen Choi, *Charity and the Letters of Barsanuphius and John of Gaza* (2020).
22. Alistair C. Stewart, *The Canons of Hippolytus. An English version, with introduction and annotation and an accompanying Arabic Text* (2021).

Εὐδώρᾳ
(again!)

# Preface

The purpose of this edition and translation of the *Canons of Hippolytus* is to provide a version for the use of students of liturgy and church history which is both accessible and responsible.

This is not the first version. Any student of this document is deeply indebted to René-Georges Coquin, who established a critical text as well as providing an introduction and a French translation. In 1987 Paul Bradshaw edited an English translation of Coquin's text by Carol Bebawi, providing brief annotation and a brief introduction. Although these works are still available, this version falls deliberately somewhere between the two. Although there is no apparatus as such (Coquin's being so thorough and complete) some important variations are given in the annotation to the translation, and notes indicate significant points of textual uncertainty, whereas the Bradshaw-Bebawi version deliberately avoids any discussion of the text, referring the reader to Coquin's edition. In particular there are occasions, such as in the discussion of post-baptismal anointing in Canon 19, where some more detailed discussion of the text is inevitable.

A text is provided because, although the work is intended for liturgical and social historians rather than Arabists, it was thought that historians with some knowledge of Arabic might benefit from the provision of a text alongside the translation; no knowledge of the language is, however, assumed, and Arabic in the footnotes to the translation is transliterated. The needs of the intended audience are further served by an introduction in which I aim to update that of Coquin, especially in the light of the renewed scrutiny of the church orders in the past years, and to include a detailed consideration of the contribution the *Canons* might make to our knowledge of early Christian liturgy. The annotations similarly focus on the relationship between the *Canons* and other church orders, as on the liturgical value of the text. Having determined that the text is Cappadocian, and perhaps linked with Eustathian circles, I was pleased and surprised to learn that Georg Kretschmar had suspected the same, although he never published any argument.

The completion of this work is the fulfilment of a long-held ambition, and so I am grateful to the assistance provided by Peter Bolt at SCD for guiding this work through the press. Since I am absolutely an amateur in the language in which this text is preserved, as in that through which it passed, I thank those with greater expertise than mine, notable among them Mohammed Basith Awan who assisted in proofreading the text, and Sacha Syed, a most patient *ustadh*. However, the greatest debt is owed to Rifaat Ebied for many corrections and suggestions regarding the text and its translation; his influence is present in every page of text and in many of the textual notes, even when he is not mentioned. As always, remaining errors and misjudgements are my responsibility alone, but thanks to him the errors are considerably fewer and the translation more assured.

My principal hope is that the provision of this version, and the assignment of the *Canons* to Cappadocian circles, will allow the evidence of this document properly to inform the ongoing exploration of early Christian liturgy and church-order.

Chalvey, Slough
On the feast of St Martin de Porres, 2020

# Contents

Introduction .................................................. 1
1. Discovery and publication .............................. 1
2. Date ........................................................ 3
3. The employment of sources in Canones Hippolyti ...... 6
   3.1    The use of Traditio apostolica ..................... 7
   3.1.1  Recastings of Traditio apostolica ................ 13
   3.1.2  Expansions of Traditio apostolica within
          the structure ..................................... 16
   3.1.3  Conclusion ....................................... 17
   3.2    Material beyond Traditio apostolica .............. 18
   3.2.1  The final Canons ................................. 18
   3.2.2  The introductory canon .......................... 23
   3.2.3  Other church order material within Canones
          Hippolyti ......................................... 24
   3.2.4  Conclusion ....................................... 32
4. The redactional purpose of Canones Hippolyti ........ 33
5. Provenance ................................................ 34
6. The liturgies of Canones Hippolyti ..................... 45
   6.1    The ordination rites .............................. 45
   6.2    The baptismal rites ............................... 47
   6.2.1  The prebaptismal rites ........................... 47
   6.2.2  The baptismal "formula" ........................ 48
   6.2.3  The baptismal creed ............................. 51
   6.2.4  The post-baptismal ceremonies .................. 53

|       |       |                                      |     |
|-------|-------|--------------------------------------|-----|
| 6.2.5 |       | Conclusion                           | 55  |
| 6.3   |       | The Pascha of Canones Hippolyti      | 56  |
| 6.4   |       | Eucharistic and other ritual meals   | 57  |
| 6.5   |       | Healing rituals                      | 60  |

7. **Conclusion** ............................................................. **61**

**Arabic Text and English Translation** ...................... **63**

**Bibliography** ............................................................. **169**

**Indices** ....................................................................... **173**

**Index locorum** .......................................................... **173**
1. Scripture ................................................................ 173
2. Ancient Christian literature ................................. 174
    2.1 Anonymous church order literature (excluding Canones Hippolyti and Traditio apostolica) ..... 174
    2.2 Conciliar canons ............................................ 175
    2.3 Other early Christian literature .................... 175
3. Other ancient sources ........................................... 176
    3.1 Literary sources ............................................. 176
    3.2 Non-literary sources ..................................... 176

**Index nominum** ....................................................... **177**

# Introduction
# The Canons of Hippolytus

## 1. Discovery and publication

The first indication of the existence of this church order is in a seventeenth century report by Vansleb, who reported the existence of 38 canons of "Abulides" in Arabic and employed in Egyptian Christian circles, though he admitted that he had no idea of the identity of this Abulides.[1] That Abulides should be identified as Hippolytus was recognized by Ludolfus.[2] However it was not until 1870 that the *editio princeps* of this Arabic text was published, with a Latin translation.[3] It was from this edition that Achelis produced a revised translation into Latin in 1891.[4] However, Haneberg had employed only two MSS in his edition, which actually, as Riedel points out, constitute a single witness, since both were taken from the same canonical collection, that of Macarius.[5] In particular this is an unfortunate witness as there is some misplacement of pages, to the extent that the final, extended, canon is misplaced and divided within the work. The correction to the order of leaves was made in a German translation published by Riedel,[6] who corrected Haneberg with reference to distinct canonical collections, namely the *Nomocanon* of

---

1 Vansleb, *Histoire de l'église d'Alexandrie*, 280–282.
2 Leutholf, *Iobi Ludolfi alias Leutholf*, 333–335. Doubt is cast on this by Baumstark, "Kanones des Hippolytos", 191–196, though the evidence is slight and the reasoning tortuous.
3 von Haneberg, *Canones S Hippolyti*.
4 Achelis, *Ältesten Quelle*. *Canones Hippolyti* is shown in columns against *Traditio apostolica* (known at the time solely from Coptic and Ethiopic witnesses) and parallel sections of *Constitutiones apostolorum* 8.
5 Riedel, *Kirchenrechtsquellen*, 196.
6 Riedel, *Kirchenrechtsquellen*, 200–230.

Michael of Damietta and a Berlin codex containing a canonical collection,[7] as well as the *Nomocanon* of Ibn al 'Assal (which is also transmitted in Ethiopic, through its inclusion in the *Fetha Nagast*, an Ethiopian canon and civil law collection) and contains material from the *Canones*. However, once the priority of *Traditio apostolica* over *Canones Hippolyti* was established, *Canones Hippolyti* remained little studied.[8] Nonetheless a critical edition (with French translation) was finally forthcoming in 1966, based on twelve MSS representing a variety of canonical collections which included *Canones Hippolyti*;[9] beyond those employed by Riedel, Coquin, the editor, observes the presence of some canons in the *Nomocanon* of Gabriel ibn Turayk (from the twelfth century), and the citation by Ibn Kabar of the contents list found in the Berlin collection in his *Miṣbāḥ al-ẓulma (Lamp of shadows)*. For the convenience of readers Coquin's text is reproduced here with minor deviations, though without the apparatus. Some reference is made to major variant readings in the English notes, but for detail the reader is referred to Coquin's work. Coquin's text was translated into English in 1987.[10]

*Canones Hippolyti* is extant solely in Arabic, though this translation is based on a Coptic original, as Coquin demonstrates on the basis of Copticisms in the Arabic text and misunderstandings of Coptic vocabulary,[11] many of which are observed in the notes to the translation presented here. This Coptic version,

---

7   Berlin *Or.* 10181, ff 51–219.
8   Achelis had been convinced that *Canones Hippolyti* was the original Hippolytean text, of which *Traditio apostolica* was a reworking. He dated the *Canones* to the early third century, though the basis of his evidence was that material which had survived from *Traditio apostolica*. The correct ordering of the documents was the work of Connolly, *So-called Egyptian Church Order* and Schwartz, *Über die pseudoapostolischen Kirchenordnungen*. Maclean, *Ancient church orders*, 141–149, came close to this position, rejecting the hypotheses of Achelis on the grounds that the *Canones* had simply retained older material.
9   Coquin, *Canons*.
10  Bradshaw, *Canons*.
11  Coquin, *Canons*, 29–31.

moreover, is based on a lost Greek original, as Coquin demonstrates on the basis of the transmission of Greek vocabulary found transliterated in the Arabic version.[12] Whereas this might simply indicate a wide Greek vocabulary on the part of a Coptic author, the number of words and their nature, including a number of Greek words which were not generally received in Coptic, indicate rather that that this is a translation of a Greek original.[13]

## 2. Date

Following the judgement, after the work of Connolly and Schwartz,[14] that *Canones Hippolyti* was a reworking of *Traditio apostolica*, rather than being its source, as Achelis had thought, this church order lay neglected until 1956, when Botte argued for a date between Nicaea and Constantinople, and for an Egyptian provenance.[15] The basis of Botte's argument for dating is the initial credal confession in *Can. Hipp.* 1, declaring the equality "in glory" of the persons of the Trinity, and the eternal pre-existence of the Son, yet avoiding the use of the *homoousion*.[16] Coquin agrees with this assessment, and that the assembly to which the canon has reference must be the council of Nicaea,[17] suggesting that the trinitarian terminology points to a date between Nicaea and Constantinople.[18] Although the council of Alexandria, should the document be of Egyptian provenance, might also be seen as a candidate for identification as the council in question, there is no mention of the discussion of the Spirit in this canon

---

12  Coquin, *Canons*, 32–33.
13  So Coquin, *Canons*, 32–33.
14  Connolly, *So-called Egyptian Church Order*; Schwartz, Über die pseudapostolischen Kirchenordnungen.
15  Botte, "Origine", 53–63.
16  Botte, "Origine", 56–57.
17  Coquin, *Canons*, 52.
18  Coquin, *Canons*, 56–57.

whereas the article regarding the Spirit in the baptismal creed,[19] whilst expanded beyond that of *Traditio apostolica*, is not as expansive as that of Alexandria, and so Nicaea remains the more obvious candidate. Coquin, indeed, suggests that had *Canones Hippolyti* been any later than the beginnings of the pneumatomachian controversy, then more would have been made of the person and status of the Holy Spirit.[20] With this we must agree. The stage of discussion, and the apparent reception of Nicaea, speaks of a stage of theological development found, for instance, in Basil *Ep*. 125, in which the Spirit is said in similar terms to be equal in glory within the Trinity, whereas the significant discussion regards the status of the Son. We might also note the baptismal formula, referring to the "equal Trinity",[21] as suggestive of a stage of development typical of the theology of the 360s. In this light we may wonder whether the council is neither Nicaea nor Alexandria, but one of the numerous councils which were convened in the fourth century to discuss the issues arising from Nicaea; since, at several points, the *Canones* seem to be negotiating provisions made in the canons of Nicaea to the extent of contradiction this must be considered possible.[22]

Pointing to a fourth century date, Coquin also observes the manner in which *Can. Hipp.* 20 and 22 describe the paschal fast and the Lenten fast as apparently independent events. This is the practice which was known in the Alexandrian church until the time of Athanasius, after which the fasts were united into a single practice. Coquin thus fixes on 340 as the latest date for *Canones Hippolyti*. This is a plausible argument, though it is also possible that the individual canons are independent in their production, and so predate the gathering of the canons into a single collec-

---

19  *Can. Hipp.* 19.
20  Coquin, *Canons*, 61.
21  *Can. Hipp.* 19.
22  See the notes on *Can. Hipp.* 9 and *Can. Hipp.* 30.

tion. We may also note that the argument assumes an Alexandrian origin. It may thus be possible to solve the issue regarding the distinction between the Lenten and paschal fast by suggesting that the Canones are not in fact Egyptian, a suggestion which will be pursued further below.

Coquin's view is to be contrasted to that of Botte, formed on the basis of the theology of the Spirit expressed both in the baptismal creed and in the addition of the term "equal Trinity" to the trinitarian baptismal formula, that the date of origin should be set between 340 and 360.[23] This seems more probable on the basis of the Trinitarian theology, though the *terminus ad quem* is again predicated on the basis of an Egyptian origin to the *Canones*, thus possibly pushing the latest possible date closer to Constantinople in 381.

Although the manner in which the Lenten and paschal fasts are distinguished perhaps indicates that the Canons had already undergone some degree of editing before being brought together in this final collection, thus making us alert to the possibility that material from distinct dates is included, in which context we may note Markschies' suggestion that the date of final redaction be put back yet further, to the end of the fourth century,[24] it seems probable that a final redactor working after Constantinople might have had particular attention to the initial canon, and in particular note its weak pneumatology, and essay corrections, which are not found. This is an indication of a date earlier in the fourth century, albeit not a strong one.

Finally, and perhaps critically, Coquin follows Botte in pointing out that the asceticism which is presupposed is not cenobitic monasticism, nor even organized eremeticism, but is something more primitive, less organized, and in touch with the local church. As such, he argues, *Canones Hippolyti* are unlikely to be a

---

23  Botte, "Origine", 59.
24  Markschies, "Wer schrieb die sogenannte *Traditio apostolica*?", 10–11.

product of the fifth century, in which period this organized monasticism came about in Egypt, but fit neatly with the practice known in the mid-fourth century.[25] We might add that the same is true of Cappadocia in the same period.

The date of final redaction may thus be set reasonably certainly somewhere between 340 and 380, though this says little about the date of the sources, and does not deal with the issue of whether multiple redactions preceded the final product. There are certainly tensions within the document, such as the assumption of distinct paschal and Lenten fasts. At this stage in the discussion, however, provenance is an open question. This issue can only be approached once the sources have been established; nonetheless, recognizing the nature of the church orders as "living literature", we may be open to the possibility that the *Canones* might have gone through multiple recensions.

### 3. The employment of sources in *Canones Hippolyti*

In turning to the manner in which *Canones Hippolyti* employs sources we may attempt to see how much is redactional construction. In what follows we assume that *Canones Hippolyti* has been transmitted in its integrity and without significant additions or alterations to the completed original.[26] Although we cannot be absolutely certain on this point, Coquin suggests that the very literal nature of the Arabic, under which the Coptic original may be discerned, would indicate that this is a justifiable working assumption.[27]

---

25  Botte, "Origine" 61–62; Coquin, *Canons*, 55–56.
26  Cf. the approach of Achelis, *Ältesten Quelle*, for whom the work is heavily interpolated. This receives severe criticism from Maclean, *Ancient church orders*, 156–158, who notes that Achelis had determined that the work had an early date on the basis of the preservation of ancient features, and then gone on to mark as an interpolation anything which tended to contradict the dating on which he had already fixed.
27  Coquin, *Canons*, 35.

## 3.1 The use of *Traditio apostolica*

The fundamental source behind *Canones Hippolyti* is *Traditio apostolica*. That *Canones Hippolyti* is a derivation from *Traditio apostolica* (as opposed to the reverse relationship) was demonstrated by Connolly.[28] Connolly demonstrated the dependent nature of *Canones Hippolyti* through observing the absence of certain passages in *Traditio apostolica* which are found in *Canones Hippolyti*, but which he considered would not be omitted by a redactor. In particular he focuses on passages which hold up the behaviour of the clergy as a means of edification and sees this as a particular concern of the compiler.[29] He also notes passages which imply that it derives from a later period than that of Hippolytus, such as the extension to the instruction regarding *grammatikoi* as catechumens (by which they are to continue in their profession, a situation which is tenable in the fourth century though not in the third) and passages which imply that a provision in *Traditio apostolica* has been misunderstood or deliberately recast by *Canones Hippolyti* (whereas the reverse relationship is unlikely) such as the manner in which the cemetery of *Traditio apostolica* is understood as a hospice by *Canones Hippolyti*, even to the extent that, in including a reference to the tiles found in its source, *Canones Hippolyti* specifies the provision of clay vessels for the sick.[30] For the greater part Connolly's argument is concerned to demonstrate the proper literary relationship between the two documents, and so we need not follow his argument in detail, not the least because of Connolly's success in stating the case; nobody now would assert that *Canones Hippolyti* is the source for *Traditio apostolica*.

However, *Canones Hippolyti* is more than simply a reworking

---

28   Connolly, *So-called Egyptian church order*, 55–59.
29   Connolly, *So-called Egyptian church order*, 61.
30   Barrett-Lennard, "Canons of Hippolytus", 159, suggests that they are used to carry provisions to the sick.

of *Traditio apostolica*; a significant amount of other material is included. However, before discussing this other material (with regard to the author's debt to other traditional material and the extent of editorial composition) we examine the use of *Traditio apostolica* in more detail.

The employment of *Traditio apostolica* may be diagrammatized thus:

| Can. Hipp. | | Trad. ap. |
|---|---|---|
| 1 | Introduction, on the faith | No direct parallel. |
| 2 | Bishops | 2 |
| 3 | Episcopal ordination and the ordination liturgy | 3–6 (much abbreviated) |
| 4 | Ordination of presbyters | 7 |
| 5 | Ordination of deacons | 8 (prayer in *Can. Hipp.* distinct from that of *Trad. ap.*) |
| 6 | Confessors | 9 |
| 7 | Appointment of readers and subdeacons | 11, 13, 12 (much rewritten and re-applied) |
| 8 | On certain charismatic phenomena | 14 |
| 9 | On presbyters relocating and on the appointment of widows | 10 (Only that part regarding widows) |
| 10 | Examination of catechumens | 15 |
| 11 | Prohibition of certain persons | 16 |
| 12 | " | 16 (cont.) |
| 13 | " | 16 (cont.) |
| 14 | " | 16 (cont.) |
| 15 | " | 16 (cont.) |
| 16 | " | 16 (cont..) |
| 17 | On the behaviour of women. | Most of the material is not in *Trad. ap.*, though the final sentence picks up *Trad. ap.* 17. |

| | | |
|---|---|---|
| 18 | Dismissal of catechumens | 18–19a (Though *Can. Hipp.* expands greatly, discussing midwives.) |
| 19 | "Baptism in blood", final catechumenal rites, baptismal liturgy. | 19b–21 |
| 20 | Instruction on fasting. | No parallel to the greater part of the Canon, though the final sentence appears to be a reworking of *Trad. ap.* 26. |
| 21 | Instruction on daily assembly. | No parallel[31] |
| 22 | Regarding the Pascha. | 33 |
| 23 | An apparent conclusion, regarding knowledge. | Some common ideas with *Trad. ap.* 1. |
| 24 | Deacons' and bishops' duties with regard to the sick. | 34 |
| 25 | Continuation of discussion of the sick-room, and times of prayer. | 40–41 |
| 26 | Prayer in the church | 41 |
| 27 | Practice of private reading and times of prayer | 41 |
| 28 | Eucharistic fasting; restriction of Communion to the baptized | 36–37 |
| 29 | Vigilance at the altar | 38–39, 42A/B |
| 30 | Instructions concerning end of catechumenate, and order of communion. | End of 21–22. Echoes of 24.1–2. |
| 31 | Deacons' role in communicating the people. | Echo of 24.1–2. |
| 32 | Fasting, widows, orphans, supper for poor. | 23, 24.3–4, 25 |
| 33 | Conduct of an *analempsis* | Echo of 26.3, 27.1, 28 |
| 34 | Conduct at table. | 28 (cont.) |
| 35 | Deacons' duties at meals | 28–30 |
| 36 | On firstfruits | 31–32 |
| 37 | Assembly of the clergy | No parallel |
| 38 | Conduct of the baptized | No parallel |

---

31  Bradshaw, *Canons*, 26, suggests that the first half of the Canon has "some affinity" with *Trad. ap.* 39. However, in discussion below it is suggested that this affinity is deceptive.

We may first observe that the first nineteen Canons follow the order of *Traditio apostolica* fairly closely and that virtually all of *Traditio apostolica* is included. That which is missing is minor and is largely covered by existing material. The order is even closer than might at first appear because there appears to be some dislocation in the Latin version, on which the chapter numbering system is based, in chapters 10–13, dealing with (in the chapter order of the Latin) widows, readers, virgins and subdeacons. The order found in the Sahidic version is 11, 13, 10, 12, (reader, subdeacon, widow, virgin) which is certainly more rational and is, moreover, close to the order of *Canones Hippolyti* (11, 13, 12, 10). It is indeed possible that *Canones Hippolyti* has preserved the original order here.

The serious difficulties with the order begin after the section on initiation concludes. However, before turning to this point we may note that there is confusion in *Traditio apostolica* itself, brought about by the existence of two conclusions. In *Traditio apostolica*, 35 is a partial doublet of 41, and there are two discussions of signing oneself with the cross, and two concluding chapters (numbered 42A and 43A, and 42B and 43B.) I have sought to answer the puzzle posed by these two conclusions by suggesting the existence of two recensions, both of which were in circulation, and bringing about a confusion which the versions, or the recensions behind the versions, sought to rationalize in various ways.[32] The two conclusions are extant, following one another, in the Latin version. Thus

Conc. 1: 34, 35, 36, 37, 38,                42A, 43A
Conc. 2: 34,                    38, 39, 40, 41, 42B, 43B

---

32  Stewart, *Hippolytus*, 39–45.

In turning to *Canones Hippolyti* we may thus observe that *Can. Hipp.* 22–27 represent *Traditio apostolica* intact, namely providing a version of *Trad. ap.* 40–41, one of the versions of the conclusion, though not extending to 42 (which is found in different versions in both conclusions.) *Can. Hipp.* 28–29 then contain a version of the other conclusion, namely *Trad. ap.* 36–39 and 42. This conclusion is rationalized by omitting 35, which is a doublet of the beginning of 41. Thus just as in the Latin version, the two conclusions are each presented, though there has been a degree of rationalization through the removal of doublets. Rather than presenting any version of the "original" conclusion to *Traditio apostolica* this witness suggests that both conclusions continued to circulate and that various redactors dealt with the confusion thus brought about in different ways.[33] The concluding chapter of each version is omitted altogether; we suggest below that the redactor of *Canones Hippolyti* has fashioned his own conclusion, and so omitted that already present.

However, although the two conclusions of *Traditio apostolica* are both found in *Canones Hippolyti*, this concluding material is misplaced. The correct order is then picked up and followed from *Can. Hipp.* 30–36. Overall, therefore the pattern of the use of *Traditio apostolica* by the redactor of *Canones Hippolyti* may be illustrated thus:

| Trad. ap. | Can. Hipp. |
|---|---|
| 1–21 | 1–19 |
| 33–42 | 22–29 |
| 22–32 | 30–36 |

On this basis we may see that the disordering is simply the result of the misplacement of a single block of material. This misplacement may be explained in one of three ways: that the redactor of

---

33  Cf. Bradshaw, *Canons*, 9.

*Canones Hippolyti* deliberately re-arranged the material, that the chapters identified as the concluding chapters are not the conclusion and *Canones Hippolyti* retains them in the correct place,[34] or that there was some misplacement and rearrangement of sheets in the copy of *Traditio apostolica* which the redactor of *Canones Hippolyti* employed.

The first explanation cannot be ruled out altogether, but a strong justification would have to be presented for this manner of proceeding, given the tendency of ancient redactors to hug the coastline of their sources very closely. No obvious explanation is at hand, and such a proceeding is all the more unlikely given that, apart from this one block of material, the order of *Traditio apostolica* is followed closely.

The second explanation is unlikely given that it does not correspond to the most complete and reliable versions of *Traditio apostolica*, namely the Latin, the Axumite Ethiopic, and the Sahidic. Moreover, as Bradshaw points out, there is a citation of Revelation 2:17 at the very end of *Trad. ap.* 21.[35] This is not found in the corresponding canon of *Canones Hippolyti* but is found in *Can. Hipp.* 30, which is the point at which, after the transplanted material, *Canones Hippolyti* picks up the order of *Traditio apostolica*. It would thus appear to be part of the misplacement. The point is that the displacement takes place within a chapter of *Traditio apostolica*, namely at the end of the chapter regarding baptism, in the discussion of catechumenate, and that the same chapter is picked up at the end of the displacement, with the citation of Revelation. This indicates that the material found in these chapters is indeed displaced, rather than reflecting a better order than *Traditio apostolica*, as the verse makes more sense in its context in *Traditio apostolica* than it does in its context in *Canones Hippolyti*. It is also noteworthy that the same

---

34  So Coquin, *Canons*, 38–39.
35  Bradshaw, *Canons*, 9.

citation of Revelation is found at the end of the baptismal material in *Canones Basilii*.[36]

Thus we should suspect the third possibility, namely accidental displacement. In support of this is the observation that in the Macarian recension parts of *Canones Hippolyti* itself underwent a process of misplacement, as noted above. We should not wonder, therefore, that a similar process might have been undergone by its source document. The most likely explanation, therefore, is that there was some accidental misplacement of pages in the text of *Traditio apostolica* employed by *Canones Hippolyti*. That the whole is a single group means that this is entirely feasible.

However, although the order of *Traditio apostolica* (as received by the redactor) is followed, much is radically recast. This is hardly a slavish following, but a re-orientation. It will be recollected that it was precisely this insight which led Connolly to the conclusion that *Traditio apostolica* was the source of *Canones Hippolyti*, rather than vice versa. Beyond the recasting of parts of *Traditio apostolica*, substantial additions are made. Thus it is at this point that we may deal in detail with the manner in which *Canones Hippolyti* rewrites its fundamental source.

### 3.1.1 Recastings of *Traditio apostolica*

We have already mentioned the analysis of *Canones Hippolyti* against *Traditio apostolica* made by Connolly. Rather than repeat Connolly's extensive work, we simply take examples illustrating the different ways in which *Canones Hippolyti* recasts its source. We have already observed that Connolly's purpose was to demonstrate that *Traditio apostolica* was anterior to *Canones Hippolyti*. This we may take for granted, but observe the recastings as ways in which the redactor worked with the material.

The first example of the redactor at work may be observed by

---

36   So Bradshaw, *Canons*, 9.

examining the distinct injunctions regarding care for the eucharistic elements in the two church orders. *Trad. ap.* 37–38, in a direction which, I have suggested, related initially to the conduct of eucharistic meals in the context of a *Sättigungsmahl*, directs that care should be taken not to drop the eucharistic bread and that no libation should be poured from the eucharistic cup.[37] I have further suggested that by the time that *Traditio apostolica* is redacted these directions are no longer understood and that such liturgical practices are already archaic. The direction regarding the cup is kept in place but that regarding the bread is retained on the understanding that this refers to the practice of retaining the eucharistic species for communion at home. Connolly is convinced that the whole passage originally referred to communion at home because it is addressed to a lay Christian (although, we may note, a lay Christian would be responsible for his or her own conduct in the eucharistic banquet.) But Connolly is certainly right to observe that in *Canones Hippolyti* the direction is addressed to clergy, and that the presumption is that the liturgy is taking place within the church. "From the indications given it is hardly possible to resist the conclusion that the complier of C.H. had in his mind's eye a picture of the altar surrounded by ministers."[38] Thus whereas *Traditio apostolica* warned against a mouse eating the eucharistic bread, which might happen to crumbs dropped from the table, or, once reservation is the issue, might happen to the eucharistic bread if it is carelessly stored, *Can. Hipp.* 29 is concerned about something climbing into the eucharistic wine.[39] The redactor clearly has no comprehension of the meaning of the original and so freely recasts the source. A similar approach is made to the eucharistic content of *Trad. ap.* 27 and 28, which is recast in order to regulate a funeral meal in

---

37 Hippolytus, 194–195.
38 Connolly *So-called Egyptian church order*, 82.
39 Or possibly something dropping. See the notes to the translation ad loc.

*Can. Hipp.* 33 and in *Can. Hipp.* 30 material from *Trad. ap.* 22, originally relating to the carrying of the *fermentum* between the churches of Rome and directing that the deacon should give the *fermentum* to the presbyter, is adapted to deal with the issue of whether a deacon should give communion to a presbyter, one which was clearly an issue in the fourth century.[40]

A contrasting example of the use of *Traditio apostolica* may be provided by the direction regarding the ordination of deacons. The introductory material is close to *Traditio apostolica*, though with the critical distinction noted below with regard to the relationship of the deacon to the other clergy, but then an entirely distinct ordination prayer is found. We may surmise that this is a prayer close to that employed in the community of *Canones Hippolyti*, though it also emphasizes the deacon's moral qualities (we have already observed, with Connolly, the interest of this redactor in the conduct of the clergy.) We may thus see that whereas the redactor of *Canones Hippolyti* wishes to be faithful to his source it is not a slavish fidelity but one with redactional purpose. It is noteworthy in this context that *Can. Hipp.* 3, regarding the Eucharist offered by the newly ordained bishop, omits the anaphora given in *Trad. ap.* 4 altogether, and that *Can. Hipp.* 4, regarding the ordination of presbyters, which in *Trad. ap.* 7 is notoriously confused due to earlier redactional involvement, recasts the material in such a way as to refer to a familiar local rite, that of seating the bishop on a teacher's chair. We may continue thus, noting once again the manner in which *Can. Hipp.* 24–5 recasts the directions of *Trad. ap.* 40 regarding the cemetery, turning this into a direction regarding the hospice. In following his source the redactor updates liturgical practice and clarifies obscurities.

---

40  That it is an issue is indicated by the fact that the 18th Canon of Nicaea legislates against such a practice.

### 3.1.2 Expansions of Traditio apostolica within the structure

Beyond following the source there are several points at which the original *Traditio apostolica* is expanded by entirely new material, usually employing catchwords. One interesting example is the addition in *Can. Hipp.* 8 to a brief chapter in *Traditio apostolica* regarding charisms,[41] which states that a presbyter is not to be excluded after his wife has given birth. This is an example of stray directions within *Canones Hippolyti* which appear to reflect the custom and concerns of the community and which are introduced at what seem to the redactor to be appropriate occasions for the insertion of material, here latching onto a mention of ordination. A similar example is provided by the expansion of *Traditio apostolica* which discussed the prayer of catechumens, made separately from that of the faithful. This remains present in *Canones Hippolyti*, but there is also a discussion of the manner in which midwives who have assisted at a birth should also be kept separate, thus latching onto the idea of separation within the community as a means of introducing this material.[42] Clearly this is a matter of concern within the community, and it is discussed at what seems to be an appropriate moment. Finally we should note the manner in which *Can. Hipp.* 20 introduces a discussion of the fasting days by picking up on a comment regarding eucharistic fasting in the original. Whether these are authorial constructions or derived from a source is hard to say. We may, however, re-iterate that these are attempts to bring the source to bear on real issues within the community to which *Canones Hippolyti* is addressed employing a simple technique of expanding the original.

This is particularly likely to be the case with regard to the transformation of the cemetery of *Traditio apostolica* into a hospice. *Trad. ap.* 34 had regard to the visit of the bishop to the sick.

---

41  *Trad. ap.* 14.
42  *Can. Hipp.* 18.

This is picked up and expanded with the statement that the steward has responsibility for the care of the sick; the discussion of the care of the sick follows, which has been reworked from a discussion in *Traditio apostolica* regarding the maintenance of the cemetery. We may assume firstly that directions regarding a cemetery had no relevance to the community of *Canones Hippolyti*, and next note that the use of catchwords has, once again, provided the occasion for the reworking of the canon. This is not simply a matter of making sure that some attention is paid to the source but is a demonstration of the central and significant place that the hospice would appear to have held in this community.

More probably employing source material, however, is the expansion of *Traditio apostolica* through the provision of the major part of *Can. Hipp.* 17, dealing with the behaviour of women; as in the case of the two examples above, this material latches onto the existing *Traditio apostolica* and expands it greatly. The moment provided is the discussion of concubinage and catechumenate. This in turn leads to a discussion of the behaviour of women more generally, particularly in church. Thus women's hairstyles are discussed, as is the wearing of jewellery and the matter of talking in church. These topics are likewise discussed within the *Sententiae* of the Council of Nicaea,[43] which is an indication that source material is being incorporated into the reworking of *Traditio apostolica*.

### 3.1.3 Conclusion

At no point is *Traditio apostolica* simply copied within *Canones Hippolyti*. It is abbreviated, when obscure or misunderstood it is rewritten, it is supplemented with new material, and it is updated liturgically. For all that, however, the redactor of *Canones*

---

43 A work which has nothing to do with the Council of Nicaea, but is a collections of sayings regarding Christian conduct deriving from the fourth century. See the notes to the translation ad loc. for parallels.

*Hippolyti* never loses sight of the coastline which he is hugging.

### 3.2 Material beyond Traditio apostolica

Quite apart from the rewritten and expanded *Traditio apostolica*, the collection is headed and concluded by Canons which are entirely without parallel and which do not fit into the structure of the original.

#### 3.2.1 The final Canons

As the redactor completes his reworking of *Traditio apostolica* two final canons are added. Their position, forming a conclusion, would indicate that these are the focus of the work overall.

The penultimate canon *(Can. Hipp.* 37) begins by discussing the assembly of the clergy, who are directed to wear white garments,[44] but extends this by suggesting that their conduct is to be more luminous than their garments.

The final canon *(Can. Hipp.* 38) begins by discussing the Pascha, and then adds to this a passage which sounds something like a homily. The discourse starts out by describing the state of those who, having renounced sin, fall back into evil ways, or who is not serious in approaching baptism. The homily then outlines the duties of a Christian. Initially the duties of all Christians are described, as the hearers are told to resemble Christ, not to commit adultery, to keep to one wife, to bring up his children. It then states that a Christian who resembles Christ will be at his right hand and will receive the crown of life. Then the discourse goes on to say: "If a Christian desires the attainment of an angelic rank he should distance himself from women once and for all..."

---

44  A provision paralleled in *Can. Athan.* 28 and *Can. Bas.* 96, though here having reference to their liturgical dress. The most striking parallel, however, is that of Gregory of Nazianzus, *Somnium de anastasiae ecclesia* 11–13 (PG37.1255) which speaks of ministers (ὑποδρηστῆρες) "standing in shining clothing, resembling the brightness of angels." The significance of this parallel will emerge below.

which leads in turn to a description of a way of life which approaches the monastic ideal, and to a discussion of the temptations of Jesus in the desert, these temptations being compared to those which might beset an ascetic.

The question is whether this discourse is from a distinct source, or whether it is a composition of the redactor of *Canones Hippolyti*. Achelis had noted various parallels between this section and other of the canons, and he is followed by Connolly. We may lay them out here:

| He shall pray and expel every evil spirit from them by his exorcism (ἐξορκισμός). They shall not return to them thenceforth through what they do. | ...for they initially said "we reject you O devil" with their mouths, and now they are rushing in his direction through their wicked deeds. |

Here we may note that the passage in *Can. Hipp.* 19, regarding baptism, is an expansion of *Traditio apostolica* by *Canones Hippolyti*, as *Traditio apostolica* (here following the Sahidic) simply states that the evil spirits flee and do not return. There is an implication here that conduct might cause the evil spirits to return, and the same is implied in *Can. Hipp.* 38. This seems, moreover, to cohere with the insight of *Canones Hippolyti* seen as central by Connolly, that the conduct of ministers is a means by which edification is brought about.

Connolly's next example also comes from the baptismal canon (*Can. Hipp.* 19):

| So they become complete Christians, nourished by the body of Christ... | Thus somebody who says "I have been baptized and received the Body of the Lord" and feels comfortable, and says "I am a Christian"... |

Once again, the section of the baptismal canon is without parallel in *Traditio apostolica*. This may be a reflection of the baptismal liturgy employed in the community of *Canones Hippolyti*, and as such may not so closely indicate common authorship, but certainly denotes a common background, implying that *Can. Hipp.* 38 is from the same redactional source as the expansions to *Traditio apostolica* in *Can. Hipp.* 19.

The other parallels are less convincing. In the discussion of women *(Can. Hipp.* 17) it is said that women should remember the Lord at all times, rather than contradicting their husbands, whereas *Can. Hipp.* 38 states that if somebody does not remember the Lord at all times then they are liable to fall into idolatry. The constant remembrance of God is a theme found elsewhere in the church order literature, and is therefore hardly a mark of common authorship between these two passages. The other parallel, between the statement that a catechumen should not be a lover of the world and the statement that a Christian likewise should not be a lover of the world is a commonplace of the church order literature.

These latter parallels, whilst not indicating common authorship, do indicate that part at least of *Can. Hipp.* 38 is redacted out of traditional material, whereas the former parallels indicate that it is certainly derived from a common community, and may well be the product of a redactor of *Canones Hippolyti*.

Achelis had suggested that this "homily" was an interpolation into what he believed to be the authentic work of Hippolytus. To an extent this impression was derived from the disordering of the leaves in Haneberg's edition. We may agree with Connolly that it is certainly integral to the *Canones*; quite apart from the strong possibility that it is the product of the redactor of the *Canones* (and not Hippolytus!), and deriving from the same background, its position as the summit of the canons is an indication that its inclusion is the fundamental purpose behind its redaction. However, the observation that traditional material is redacted into the "homily" is significant.

In examining the first part of the canon, the weight of material with contact with the two ways tradition is impressive. Such a weight of parallels indicates that it is drawing on a catechetical tradition. The parallels are noted in the translation, but here we may give a flavour:

> Because the Christian should be one who walks in the path of the commandments of Christ, conformed to God as beloved children, conformed to Christ in every regard. He does not speak evil (cf. *Did.* 2.3), and nor is he a fornicator (*Did.* 2.2), nor scornful, nor a slanderer, nor a faultfinder (*Did.* 2.3). He is not corrupt, nor longs for what is perishable. He is not obstinate, nor a lover of gain (*Did.* 3.5), nor haughty (*Did.* 3.3), nor a grumbler (*Did.* 3.6), nor pronouncing judgement in matters which are not his concern (*Did.* 2.6), nor spending his inheritance where there is no salvation, nor labouring at what is not proper, nor unmerciful (*Did.* 3.8), nor bearing false witness (*Did.* 2.3), nor should he be someone who loves honour, nor should he be quarrelsome (*Did.* 3.2), nor a drunkard.

This need not make it catechesis, as it may simply be a reminder of the content of catechesis; insofar as it goes on to advice for more advanced Christian practice, it may be functioning as an introduction to the Christian life. As such it may be compared to the pseudo-Athanasian *Fides patrum* and the closely related *Syntagma Doctrinae* which use a version of the two ways tradition to introduce rules for urban monastics.[45] The principal concern of this canon, however it be classified, is the encouragement of appropriate behaviour by all in the church. Insofar as this is the purpose of much of the additional material, we may see this as the fundamental concern of the redactor.

Such a concern may also relate to a notable theme within *Canones Hippolyti* which is not found much elsewhere in the Church order tradition, namely the concern with ritual purity. Indeed, *Didascalia apostolorum* is in part a polemic against what

---

45  See, for these, Stewart, *On the two ways*, 121–146.

it perceives as a Judaizing approach to ritual purity, whereas Coquin observes what he calls a "Judaizing" tendency in *Canones Hippolyti*.[46] He notes *Can. Hipp.* 18, with the restatement of levitical purity both for women and for their midwives after childbirth, as well as minor adjustments to regulations regarding candidates for baptism found in *Traditio apostolica*. Thus when it is stated in *Trad. ap.* 16.8 that a soldier who might kill should not be accepted, *Can. Hipp.* 13 clarifies that a soldier might be bound with the "sin of blood", and that purification (in the form of what would seem to be a penitential process) should be undergone.[47] It moreover clarifies *(Can. Hipp.* 19) the requirement of *Trad. ap.* 20.6 for the postponement of the baptism of a menstruating woman by stating that she should wait until she is purified. This is reminiscent of the approach of Dionysius of Alexandria with regard to the communion of women who are in their menses,[48] but even more directly of Timothy of Alexandria's direction that a woman in menses should not be baptized until she be "purified".[49] There is also a statement that a presbyter is not to be excluded after his wife's childbirth, again indicating a concern for ritual purity within the community to which the canons are addressed. There does not seem to be any evidence here to indicate a Jewish provenance on the part of the author, as Coquin suggests,[50] but rather that purity laws ultimately derived from forming Judaism continue to be known and valued in this community.

The statement regarding the status of a soldier, however, is interesting, as it is similar to a comment not much earlier, dis-

---

46 Coquin, *Canons*, 52–53.
47 Perhaps similar to the proposal of Basil *Ep.* 188.13, that a soldier who has killed in war should abstain from Communion for three years.
48 *Ad Basileiden* 2.
49 *Resp. can.* 6.
50 Coquin, *Canons*, 53, a suggestion with which Hanssens, "Édition critique", 540, concurs.

cussing other trades and professions forbidden to Christians, based on provisions originally found in *Traditio apostolica*, in which, once again, the language of purification is employed. The ethical interest of the redactor of *Canones Hippolyti* is clear throughout; what is interesting here is that the language and conception of a period of purification is employed to describe the penitential process. It is not so much a matter of purity being redefined as ethical, rather than ritual, but ritual itself is redefined and employed to bring about ethical purity.

### 3.2.2 The introductory canon

The other significant part of *Canones Hippolyti* without parallel in *Traditio apostolica* is the introductory *Can. Hipp.* 1, connecting the profession of a Trinitarian faith to what follows, as to the living of a Christian life. Bradshaw points out that *Canones Basilii* likewise begin with such a doctrinal introduction[51] and we may note the same of the *Syntagma Doctrinae*, a monastic rule from fourth century Egypt, which, although not related to the Hippolytean stream of tradition is related to the church order tradition through the use of material deriving from the two-ways tradition and other material found within the church orders. The manner in which Christian life and conduct is related to doctrinal accuracy in the statement of Christian faith seems to be an emerging theme within the literature and the tradition.

It is also to be noted that this introductory canon turns the following material into fictive canons of this council. As such it does much what *Apostolic church order* does, and *Const. ap.* 8.4 onward, in creating a fictional council, here, apparently, either the Council of Nicaea or one of the other fourth-century councils, rather than a gathering of apostles, and turning the church-order material that follows into canons of that council.

---

51  Bradshaw, *Canons*, 11.

### 3.2.3 Other church order material within Canones Hippolyti

Coquin suggests, given that *Traditio apostolica* was transmitted as part of a collection of church orders, that the redactor might have had these at hand, and that some attention is paid to them.[52] We need to enquire whether this is indeed the case or whether, given that *Traditio apostolica* was not always simply part of a collection but had at one point been a freestanding document, the apparent echoes of other church order material reflect the tradition, rather than a relationship of literary dependence.

Coquin argues that the picture of the perfect Christian set out in the concluding *Can. Hipp.* 38 is inspired by the first part of *Apostolic church order*, and that *Can. Hipp.* 26, stating that the Christian should hurry to church is comparable to of *Apostolic church order* 11.[53] Similarly he suggests that *Can. Hipp.* 22, which discusses the manner in which Christians should bear suffering in imitation of that of the Lord is comparable to a section of *Didasc. ap.* 19,[54] and also notes the similarity of the paschal provision within this Canon to *Didasc. ap.* 21.[55]

We deal first with the alleged parallels to *Apostolic church order*. It must be admitted in the first instance that there is material in *Canones Hippolyti* which is reminiscent in some manner of *Apostolic church order*, but there is no structural similarity between the two, which makes direct literary dependence a most unlikely explanation of the relationship. We may rather suggest that the echoes in *Canones Hippolyti* are echoes of the two-ways tradition, a common ancestor of *Apostolic church order* and *Didache*, apart from other manifestations, including manifesta-

---

52  Coquin, *Canons*, 41.
53  Coquin, *Canons*, 41.
54  *Didasc. ap.* 5.5.4–6 (part of chapter 19 of the Syriac).
55  Coquin, Canons, 41–42 with reference to *Didasc. ap.* 5.18b–5.19.1 (part of the chapter 21 in the Syriac). Connolly, *So-called Egyptian church order*, 76–77, also considers it probable that the provisions regarding the Pascha are derived from *Didascalia apostolorum*.

tions within the monastic literature of fourth-century Egypt.[56] Thus whereas we may, for instance, compare the statement of *Can. Hipp.* 26 that the Lord, where his majesty is remembered, causes his spirit to dwell there with the statement of *Apostolic church order* 12 that "inasmuch as the dominion is discussed, the Lord is there" we may observe that this is also found in *Did.* 4.1. The statements in *Apostolic church order* that a Christian should not be an adulterer, a grumbler, should not be lazy, should bring up his children in the fear of the Lord, which, among others, may readily be paralleled from the two ways sections both of *Apostolic church order* and the *Didache*, may be explained, very simply, as above, by suggesting that the canon here is referring to the content of catechesis, especially given that this section is discussing those who are recently baptized, and that the content of catechesis, the *Sitz im Leben* for the generation of the two ways, is derived from the same traditional paraenesis. Thus in illustrating that point above, although *Didache* parallels were given, this was not intended to suggest a direct literary relationship, but simply to use the *Didache* as an early and accessible representative of the two ways tradition.

The alleged parallels with *Didascalia apostolorum* are even less certain. The first alleged parallel is between *Didasc. ap.* 5.5.4–6 and the statement in *Can. Hipp.* 22 that, given that the Lord had suffered for us, we should accept some share in his suffering. The context, however, is utterly distinct, as *Didascalia apostolorum* is speaking of persecution whereas *Canones Hippolyti* is speaking of fasting.

The rest of the alleged parallel between *Didascalia apostolorum* and *Canones Hippolyti*, also in *Can. Hipp.* 22, consists, according to Coquin, of the diet of bread, salt and water recommended by the Canon for the Pascha. He also suggests that the

---

56  Namely the *Syntagma doctrinae* and the *Fides patrum*. See Stewart, *On the two ways*, 121–146.

provisions of *Can. Hipp.* 38, that nobody is to sleep, is also a derivation of the paschal provisions of the *Didascalia*. Both these provisions are found in the same small section of *Didascalia apostolorum*, namely 5.18b–5.19.1. This chapter of *Didascalia apostolorum* is a complex mosaic of sources and redactions. I have previously argued that this part of *Didascalia apostolorum* is redactional, and originally intended to "de-Quartodecimanize" a Quartodeciman source.[57] It may well reflect the (?third)-century practice of that particular redactor, but as such the parallel is hardly a literary parallel, but simply an indication that the fasting practice and manner of keeping the night of Pascha had some common ground. Indeed, *Canones Hippolyti* is far less explicit about the period in which the bread and salt diet is to be kept up, for according to *Didascalia apostolorum* this is for the first part of the week only, and that the fast should become absolute thereafter. This is not to say that this canon does not have some source lying behind it because, as Coquin himself notes,[58] the paschal calculation employed is not that found in Egypt, but the source is not *Didascalia apostolorum* but is either entirely independent or a mark of some reworking of *Traditio apostolica* before it came into the hands of the redactor of *Canones Hippolyti*. Most importantly we may note that the justification for the paschal fast differs. For *Canones Hippolyti* it is a matter of sharing the suffering of Christ, whereas for *Didascalia apostolorum* the paschal fast is a vicarious fast for the Jews. It happens that both explanations of the fast are found in Quartodeciman circles, the practice of fasting having derived from Israelite Passover fasting, and the justifications offered thus developing subsequently.[59]

We thus conclude that there is no literary relationship between

---

57  Stewart, *Didascalia apostolorum*, 33–44. Similarly seeing a Quartodeciman source behind this section is Rouwhorst, *Les hymnes pascales*, 164–183.
58  Coquin, *Canons*, 62.
59  See, for some discussion, Stewart-Sykes, *The Lamb's high feast*, 160–163.

*Canones Hippolyti* and *Didascalia apostolorum*, or between *Canones Hippolyti* and *Apostolic church order*.[60] It is significant, however, that elements of the common tradition, in particular the two ways, are found in *Canones Hippolyti*, even as *Apostolic church order* has used a two-ways document as a direct source. We may also suggest that the paschal Canon is Quartodeciman in origin, thus employing an Asian method for calculating the time of the Pascha, and referring to a justification for the paschal fast with a recognizably Quartodeciman ancestry. As already noted, this stands in tension to the canon regarding fasting, which simply mentions Lent, taken as inclusive of the paschal fast.

There are, however, other echoes of other material from the relatives of the church order tradition. Thus Riedel points out the similarity between certain of the directions regarding the hours of prayer and those in the ps-Athanasian *De virginitate*.[61] Coquin responds that these are hardly unique, and are found in *Traditio apostolica*.[62] We may concur that this is an example of the transmission of tradition. However, Coquin also lays out the other passages observed by Riedel which might indicate some common ground between the treatise and *Canones Hippolyti*.

At *Virg.* 7 the virgin undertaking a voluntary fast is told to avoid the love of money. Similar directions are found in the homiletic passage addressed to the ascetic in *Can. Hipp.* 38. Riedel's next example also parallels the advice to the ascetic in the homiletic section since *Virg.* 8, as does *Can. Hipp.* 38, advises the ascetic not to take pride in virtue. Similarly *Virg.* 22 directs that the ascetic should wash the feet of the saints, in a similar manner again to *Can. Hipp.* 38. The final example is not from *Can, Hipp.* 38 but from *Can. Hipp.* 27, which is advice to read if there is no

---

60  Hanssens, "Édition critique", 539, though without a detailed treatment, suggests the same conclusion.
61  Riedel, "Bemerkungen", 338–342.
62  Coquin, *Canons*, 43.

assembly. This, however, is derived from *Traditio apostolica*, and the parallel is rather inexact. It is, however, also found elsewhere in ascetic literature, and so we may have the source here for its reception into later ascetic literature.

Riedel and Coquin do not pronounce on the relationship between the works, but it seems certain that *Can. Hipp.* 38 is incorporating traditional material in the same way that *De virginitate* does. It would not be unreasonable to suggest that *Can. Hipp.* 38 is drawing on a common fund, whether written or oral, circulating in the same area and period. However, we may also suggest that this common fund, and possibly even the homily on which *Can. Hipp.* 38 is based, is not Egyptian but, like *De virginitate* itself, Cappadocian.[63]

Such an impression of a common fund is strengthened if one were to note the other parallels observed by Coquin from the writings of Evagrius Ponticus and the *Sententiae* of Nicaea.

The first noted by Coquin is the advice to virgins to read at the rising of the sun, and turn to work after the second hour, found in Evagrius, as in the *Sententiae*,[64] which Coquin considers parallel to *Can. Hipp.* 27. This, however, would seem to be an ascetic reworking of the ancient rule. The other, however, is striking indeed. It is between the opening of Evagrius' *De malignis cogitationibus* and *Can. Hipp.* 38. Evagrius starts by discussing the three demons who stand in the way of askesis, which are said to be those entrusted with the appetites of gluttony, those that inspire us to love money, and those that entice us to seek human glory. These three fundamental demonic influences are then compared to the three temptations undergone by Jesus, the temptation that stones might be turned to bread, that of worshipping the Devil,

---

63  On the Cappadocian origin of this *De virginitate*, previously attributed to Athanasius, see Aubineau, "Les écrits", 144–151. Riedel had thought *Virg.* to be Egyptian, and so employed the parallels to argue for an Egyptian provenance.
64  Evagrius *Sent. ad Virg.* 4; *Sent. Conc. Nic.* 6.5.

and that of throwing himself from the Temple pinnacle. This first temptation is given two interpretations, namely that alien thoughts should intrude when one is fasting, or else that it is an indication that one might be tempted to turn to love of money (it is this latter which also appears in *De virginitate.*) The second temptation (the Temple pinnacle) is interpreted as a source of pride and vainglory. The final temptation, that of worshipping the Devil, is taken as a warning against falling into idolatry.[65]

The parallels with *Can. Hipp.* 38 are striking. The same three fundamental temptations are mentioned, albeit in a different order, and the same linkage is made to the temptations of Jesus. The same interpretation of the temptations, moreover, is given. Finally, and perhaps obviously, this material is addressed to ascetics. Coquin points out that the same treatment of the temptations of Christ is found in John Cassian *Conf.* 5.[66] He concludes that the version in *Canones Hippolyti* is the least developed, however of the discussions, and is therefore most likely to be earliest. One cannot help but agree, in particular given the other evidence which indicates a date for *Canones Hippolyti* in the middle of the fourth century. The indications are either that *Canones Hippolyti* is a source for the Evagrian material or, given the linkage with *De virginitate,* that *Canones Hippolyti,* for all that it is a redactional composition, is drawing upon a forming ascetic tradition into which Evagrius had also tapped.

There is, moreover, a further Evagrian parallel in *Can. Hipp.* 38, in the description of the ascetic as one who aspires to be of angelic rank. Evagrius' terminology is comparable, as he describes the monk who attains true prayer while yearning for the heavenly father's face as ἰσάγγελος,[67] describes the contemplative as one who

---

65 Evagrius *De malignis cogitationibus* 1.
66 Coquin, *Canons,* 47.
67 Evagrius *Or.* 113.

engages in angelic practice,[68] and characterizes prayer for others as an imitation of the "angelic mode" (ἀγγελικὸν... τρόπον).[69] Whereas these Evagrian parallels might point to an Egyptian provenance, we must remember the Pontic origin of Evagrius, and his time spent with Basil and Gregory, and wonder whether *Can. Hipp.* 38, with its Evagrian echoes, in fact reflects an Asian asceticism being brought to Egypt, rather than a native Egyptian spirituality. Such must be considered possible in view of Asian documents comparing the prayer life of ascetics to the life of heaven. Such a tradition emerges, Frank suggests, out of forming Judaism, and in a Syrian and Asian milieu,[70] again indicating that the origins of *Canones Hippolyti* perhaps do not lie in Egypt, but in the area north and west of Antioch. We may also note that the angelic life is mentioned in *De virginitate*, a parallel observed by Riedel, in stating that fasting is ἀγγέλων βίος.[71]

A further source of parallels, however, is provided by the *Sententiae* of Nicaea. As Coquin remarks,[72] a good number of these have the appearance of being born of the same spirit as *Canones Hippolyti*. He lists the following:

The prohibition on women wearing jewellery to church *(Can. Hipp.* 17) is comparable to *Sent. Conc. Nic.* 4.3 which states that for a woman to dress herself in jewellery to go to church is idolatrous. The prohibition within this canon on women wearing wavy hair or fringes is likewise found in *Sent. Conc. Nic.* 4.5. It is to be noted that this canon is largely without parallel within *Traditio apostolica*.

The instruction that one is to take up a book and read when there is no service in church *(Can. Hipp.* 27) is paralleled by *Sent. Conc. Nic.* 6.5 which states that a book should be taken up and

---

68 Or. 142.
69 Or. 40.
70 Frank, ΑΓΓΕΛΙΚΟΣ ΒΙΟΣ, 198–201 in conclusion.
71 *Virg.* 7; observed by Riedel, "Bemerkungen", 341.
72 Coquin, *Canons*, 48.

read by a virgin on awaking. It is to be noted that this is likewise a direction to be found in *De virginitate*, and that it was suggested above that this is a development from *Traditio apostolica*. The parallel is inexact.

The description of a man who marries another other than his concubine (especially if the concubine has a child by him) as a murderer and infanticide (*Can. Hipp.* 16) is paralleled by the characterization of an adulterer in *Sent. Conc. Nic.* 7.1 as "worthless, and an infanticide". Again, there may be a literary relationship here, as the *Sententiae* seem to have lost the sense of why such a one might be described as an infanticide.

The direction at *Can. Hipp.* 21 that a latecomer is to be excluded is paralleled by a statement in the *Sententiae* that any who is late without good cause (ἀνάγκη) lacks the blessing.[73]

The direction to offer firstfruits at *Can. Hipp.* 32 is paralleled by a like direction in the *Sententiae*.[74] However, this again is ultimately a direction derived from *Traditio apostolica*, although it is expanded in an interesting manner in *Canones Hippolyti*.

Coquin concludes that it is difficult to determine a direct dependence of the *Sententiae* on the *Canones*, but that the two reflect the same ecclesiastical background and possibly the same period in the religious situation which they suppose, and in the moral and disciplinary tendencies which they represent. This is borne out by my recent examination of the *Sententiae*, which concludes that they are a product of Egyptian Nicene circles in the middle of the fourth century;[75] however, there is other material within the *Sententiae* with parallels elsewhere in the church order literature. I may suggest that the parallels regarding the dress of women, and the characterization of an adulterer as a murderer, reflect a common tradition, though elsewhere it would

---

73  Sent. Conc. Nic. 8.14.
74  Sent. Conc. Nic. 15.7.
75  Stewart, *Gnomai*.

be unwise to overemphasize the common ground between the two documents. What is notable about these parallels is that they are expansions of *Traditio apostolica* material.

Finally we may note the close relationship between the material additional to *Traditio apostolica* in *Can. Hipp.* 29 and *Can. Bas.* 96, detailed in the notes to the translation. It is hard to evaluate this; possibly there has been literary borrowing (though the *Canones Basilii* are agreed to be later, in which case the borrowing if from *Canones Hippolyti*), and possibly this is an interpolation in *Canones Hippolyti* from the same source as *Canones Basilii*. The *Canones Basilii* are not Egyptian in origin,[76] but may have been extended in Egypt, and so we cannot be sure of the source of this material, though one suspects it is not Egyptian. The literary overlap should be observed, but we can do little more than observe it.

### 3.2.4 Conclusion

Material with parallels in the church order literature beyond *Traditio apostolica* is employed to supplement the source, and much of this has linkages with the later ascetic literature of Egypt and Cappadocia; it does not appear, however, that there is any direct derivation of material from the classical church orders. As such we may see this as a growth within the tradition, as more generally catechetical material is developed for use by ascetics. The same process may be observed in the manner in which the *Syntagma Doctrinae* and the *Fides Patrum* redeploy the two ways tradition as an introduction to ascetic directions, and the *Apostolic Church Order* as an introduction to a discussion of ministries in the church.

---

76   Camplani &Contardi, "Remarks", 139–159, in the most recent treatment of this text, suggest an Antiochene origin.

## 4 The redactional purpose of Canones Hippolyti

On the basis of the identification of the sources of *Canones Hippolyti* we may turn to the fundamental question, posed equally by all the church order documents, that of attempting to discern a rationale behind the rewriting of an existing, complete and circulating church order.

Some insight may come through observing a minor but significant divergence between *Canones Hippolyti* and the Latin text of *Traditio apostolica*. In the episcopal ordination prayer the Latin, supported by the Ethiopic, states that the Father bestowed a spirit of leadership on Christ, which he, in turn, had bestowed on the apostles. In *Canones Hippolyti* the spirit is that of Christ by nature. Assuming here that the Latin reflects the original, and is not an "Arianizing" alteration to the text, we may see the redactor of *Canones Hippolyti* seeking to avoid any indication of subordinationism. In this light we may observe the statement of Trinitarian theology in the prologue, effectively replacing the original prologue. The original in turn appears, much altered, in *Can. Hipp.* 23, in which, although there is little verbal parallel, the ideas expressed are readily comparable to those expressed in the introduction to *Traditio apostolica*.[77] So we suggest a deliberate movement of the original prologue undertaken in order to replace it with a statement of Trinitarian theology.

The pursuit of doctrinal orthodoxy is seen in the *Fides patrum* as intimately linked to the conduct of believers,[78] and this

---

77   Bradshaw, *Canons*, 27, points out that the introduction to *Traditio apostolica* is found, likewise misplaced, in the Ethiopic version, thus suggesting that the redactor of *Canones Hippolyti* might have found the chapter in that position, and adapted it to his purpose. Cf. however our suggestion immediately below.
78   Thus *Fides patrum* 1: "The way of life of that catholic church, and especially of bishops and clerks and monastics and other Christians and of all their sons. They should command firstly in this way, directing and stating thus: that we are saved by grace, but grace desires that her own children should be self-selected and sons of wisdom, and tested in every good deed, to be zealous for the good and so to act, manifestly to make themselves worthy of that correct faith"

is an insight which *Canones Hippolyti* would seem to share, as opposed to the concerns of the original *Traditio apostolica* that doctrinal orthodoxy should be guarded by proper ecclesial organization. As such we may see the logic by which *Canones Hippolyti* takes the provisions of *Traditio apostolica* and strengthens the provisions regarding the conduct of the clergy through the emphasis, in the ordination prayers, on clergy as an example but most especially in the penultimate *Can. Hipp.* 37 focussing on the manner in which the ethical conduct of the clergy is mirrored in the liturgy and, in particular through the provision of the concluding address, regarding the conduct of the faithful.

The presentation of a church which is pure both in doctrine and in ethics, and the communication of this purity to individual Christians, may be seen as the fundamental purpose behind the redaction of these canons. Their hearer is to grow in holiness, as is the church.

## 5 Provenance

The question of provenance has been put aside until after the examination of the contents.

Previous discussions have tended to assume an Egyptian provenance.[79] Early discussions, leading to this conclusion, may, however, be put aside, since they presume that *Canones Hippolyti* is a source of *Traditio apostolica* and the earliest stage of this chain of material.[80] However, Coquin argues for this on the basis of the clear literary tradition binding *Canones Hippolyti* to other works of Egyptian provenance or influence, such as the *Sententiae* of

---

79  The only exceptions of which I am aware are a brief comment by Kretschmar, "Beiträge zur Geschichte der Liturgie", 1-54, 38-39, suggesting that the *Canones* are Asian, and Achelis, *Ältesten Quellen*, who believed the *Canons* to be the work of Hippolytus of Rome.
80  Thus, e.g., Morin, "L'origine", 241-46, who suggests that Dionysius of Alexandria is the author!

Nicaea as well as the fact that the work has survived solely in Egyptian canonical collections,[81] and is followed, rather blindly, by Hanssens.[82] He does, however, note the counter-argument that *Can. Hipp.* 22 fixes the Pascha in accordance with Jewish calculations, which, he notes, were not employed in the Alexandrian method of fixing the Pascha. He suggests, however, that this canon is simply taken over from *Didascalia apostolorum*,[83] a suggestion which we have seen to be highly improbable. This, indeed, alerts us to the possibility that even if the final collection is Egyptian, its sources are not necessarily so.

In favour of Egyptian provenance we may also note two observations of Connolly on *Can. Hipp.* 36.[84] This is a reworking of *Traditio apostolica*, which likewise makes provision for the offering of firstfruits, but the prayer found in *Canones Hippolyti* is distinct from that within *Traditio apostolica*. Connolly observes that there are two verbal echoes within this prayer of the Egyptian liturgy of St Mark:

| Can. Hipp. | Mark |
| --- | --- |
| Bless Lord, the crown of the year, which is your bounty, and may they satisfy the poor of your people. | Bless, Lord, the crown of the year of your goodness, for the poor of your people.[85] |
| Your servant, N, who has brought these things, which are yours, because he fears you, bless him from your holy heaven, and all his house, and pour upon him your holy mercy... | We set before you from your own gifts; and we pray and beseech you, for you are good and love man, send out from your holy height, from your prepared dwelling place, from your unbounded bosom, the Paraclete himself, the Holy Spirit...[86] |

---

81  Coquin, *Canons*, 61–63.
82  Hanssens, "Édition critique", 540.
83  Coquin, *Canons*, 62–63.
84   Connolly, *So-called Egyptian church order*, 120–121.
85  Cited from the version at Jasper & Cuming, *Prayers of the Eucharist*, 61.
86  Jasper & Cuming, *Prayers of the eucharist*, 65.

Since I have argued elsewhere that Egyptian anaphoras are built out of individual euchological elements,[87] it is not inconceivable that some of these might be found in such diverse sources. As Connolly points out, the citation of Ps 65:11 (64:12), whereas found more widely, is in both instances linked to the idea of the support of the poor (the latter idea, linked to creation and thanksgiving, also being found extant in the Strasbourg fragment.) Connolly points out that there are two items of common ground between the epiclesis of Mark and the continuation of the prayer in *Canones Hippolyti*, namely the notion that the gifts are already the Lord's before being offered, and the petition that grace be sent from on high. Whereas this liturgical common ground may be an indication of an Egyptian provenance for *Canones Hippolyti*, this may simply indicate that this individual canon had received an Egyptian redaction.

Concurring with the idea of Egyptian provenance, Brakmann nonetheless suggests that we should not tie *Canones Hippolyti* too closely to Alexandria. In particular he points to the provisions of *Can. Hipp.* 37 for a gathering with the bishop and the clergy, and suggests that such a thing was not native to Alexandria; he points out that when the congregations gathered under Athanasius in 359 this was a departure from any previous practice, whereas the gathering envisaged in *Canones Hippolyti* is a regular event, and on this basis proposes an Egyptian provenance beyond Alexandria.[88] Similarly he observes that the assumption of the *Canones* is that the bishop should celebrate with the clergy and communicate the people, whereas in Alexandria the individual presbyters celebrated in their churches;[89] indeed he suggests that the degree of autonomy of the individual presbyters in the Alexandrian church is simply not reflected in the *Canones*,

---

87  Stewart, *Two early Egyptian liturgical papyri*.
88  Brakmann, "Alexandreia und die Kanones des Hippolyt", 146–147.
89  Brakmann, "Alexandreia und die Kanones des Hippolyt", 146.

as one would expect them to be.[90] It may, however, equally well reflect a situation in which bishops are still effectively heads of single congregations, and thus that the gathering is simply the regular gathering of a single church for worship with its bishop. Such a context is not known in Egypt, but still known in fourth century Cappadocia, as *Testamentum Domini* and *Apostolic church order* bear witness.

According to Coquin a further point indicating a possible Egyptian, and fourth century, provenance is provided by the indications that monepiscopate is a relatively recent emergence; however monepiscopate with a subordinate presbyterate emerged in Alexandria around the turn of the third century, though the Alexandrian presbyters continued to be a significant force into the fourth century. As such we may examine what is said of presbyters and bishops to see whether this might indicate an Alexandrian provenance. First we may note that at *Can. Hipp.* 2 "one of the bishops and presbyters" is selected to say the ordination prayer for the new bishop (as opposed to the provision of *Trad. ap.* 2.5 that one of the bishops should say it), and next may observe *Can. Hipp.* 4, derived from *Trad. ap.* 7.1, which states that at the ordination of a presbyter one is to pray the same prayer as for the ordination of a bishop, as "the presbyter is equal to the bishop in everything apart from the throne and ordination". The direction regarding the prayer is derived (though also adapted) from *Traditio apostolica* but the explanation is not. We may also note that in *Can. Hipp.* 5 the deacon is said to be the servant of the bishop and the presbyters in everything, as against *Trad. ap.* 8.2, which states that the deacon is to serve the bishop; this is an indication of a powerful presbytery, though does not necessarily indicate that monepiscopate is a recent development. All of this coheres with what is known in Alexandria, where we may note

---

90 Brakmann, "Alexandreia und die Kanones des Hippolyt", 145.

the possibility that the bishop was seated as part of the ordination rite.[91] Beyond Alexandria very little is known of Egyptian ecclesiastical organization; thus whereas Brakmann may be right that *Canones Hippolyti* emerges from Egypt beyond Alexandria, this is far from assured. Seating of the bishop is, moreover, known beyond Egypt,[92] and an effective aggregation of the episcopate to the presbyterate, like that seen in *Canones Hippolyti*, emerges from *Testamentum Domini* and *Apostolic church order*,[93] which are Cappadocian. As such, far from indicating an Egyptian origin, the relationship between bishop and presbyters envisaged by *Canones Hippolyti* is more indicative of a Cappadocian provenance.

This observation joins with others above, such as the possibly Cappadocian origin of the Evagrian language in *Can. Hipp.* 38, and the Quartodeciman origin of the paschal timetable, which might indicate that *Canones Hippolyti* is not native to Egypt.

Perhaps critical for such a discussion is the regulation of the κοιμητήριον in *Can. Hipp.* 24–25.

The subject arises as an expansion of Hippolytean material regarding the visit of the bishop to the sick.[94] The original is expanded through a suggestion that the bishop might offer healing while he is there. It then goes on to suggest that the sick should not lie in at the κοιμητήριον, but only the poor. The chapter regarding the cemetery is then reworked, by taking the κοιμητήριον as a sick-room, and regulating the appointment of a steward to take care of the sick. The clay tiles which were, in the original, to seal the *loculi* of graves, are taken to be pots, which

---

91  The evidence is not, however, as strong as it is in Syria and Asia, being largely limited to a hint in Synesius *Ep.* 67, and a tale told by Liberatus *Brev.* (PL68. 1036–1037A) of a disputed election in which the hand of a dead bishop was employed prior to seating.
92  In Antioch (*Const. ap.* 8.5), in Syria more widely (ps-Clem. *Ad Jac.* 5; *Hom.* 3.60–72) and in Asia (*Vit. Pol.* 22).
93  This understanding is to be preferred to Hanssens' simple statement that the redactor has "tendances presbytérales très marqueés" ("Édition critique", 539).
94  *Trad. ap.* 34.

the bishop is to supply to the steward.

The mention of such concern for the sick, and the indication that the community producing the *Canons* had a place of hospitality under an appointed steward, leads one to ask what is known of Christian care for the sick, and of Christian hospitality for the poor, in the fourth century. Dionysius, in an earlier period, reported the activities of Christians in the plague of Alexandria,[95] indicating a general concern for the sick in Christian circles, but the first evidence of such organized concern is found in the fourth century. The same organization, we may note, extended to concern for the poor and for hospitality more generally. Christians had historically concerned themselves with the poor, and hospitality is seen as a virtue, but this is dependent on the clergy, and is largely internal.

We know of *xenodochia* in Antioch in 332 through a report that Constantine had provided an allowance to the churches of Antioch for the provision of the poor in the *xenodochia*.[96] Although this source is perhaps unreliable,[97] it is not long after that we hear of Leontius of Antioch in 360 appointing men to manage *xenodochia*.[98] Further evidence of the operation of *xenodochia* in Antioch is provided by Chrysostom in the 380s.[99] In Constantinople we hear from Sozomen of a deacon called Marathonius, "a zealous superintendent (ἐπίτροπος) of the hospices for the poor (πτωχείων... συνοικιῶν) and the monastic houses of men and women,"[100] and of Constantius' provision for

---

95  Eusebius *Hist. Eccl.* 7.22.1–11.
96  Theophanis *Chronographia* 5824.
97  Horden, "Poverty", 723, thinks this source too late to be reliable. Cf. Miller, *The birth of the hospital*, 21, who finds this credible.
98  *Chronicon Paschale* 350.
99  *Ad Stagirium* 3.13 (PG47.490); *Hom.* 33 in Hebr. 13.4 (PG63. 227–228); moreover we may note that Theodoret *Hist. Eccl.* 5.18.2–5 speaks of the Empress Placilla's activity in visiting the sick in the ξενῶνες of the churches of Antioch.
100 Sozomen, *Hist. Eccl.* 4.20.2.

hospices in the city.¹⁰¹ Most notable, however, is the organizational effort of Basil in Cappadocia.¹⁰² His foundation, the Basileias, is described by Sozomen as the "most celebrated hospice for the poor (ὁ πτωχῶν... καταγώγιον),"¹⁰³ and Gregory Nazianzen as a "new city."¹⁰⁴ Basil himself describes it as a complex of buildings around a church, meeting the needs of those travelling, and of those in need,¹⁰⁵ and elsewhere characterizes it as a πτωχοτροφεῖον.¹⁰⁶ It is indeed possible that Basil was influenced in this respect by the activity of Eustathius, who had established a πτωχοτροφεῖον in Sebaste;¹⁰⁷ although Horden doubts this line of influence,¹⁰⁸ he does note that much of the evidence for the establishment of hospices in the fourth century seem to derive from Eustathian circles,¹⁰⁹ and that the fourth century evidence is limited to Constantinople, Antioch, and the cities in between. For this area, however, the evidence is extensive. Thus Julian charges Arsacius, the high priest of Galatia, to establish hostels (ξενοδοκεῖα), in order that strangers (ξένοι) "may benefit from our benevolence (φιλανθρωπία)"¹¹⁰ as a means of beating the Christians at the game they had themselves invented.

We may contrast this provision to the lack of provision in Edessa, which necessitated Ephrem's assumption of responsibility.¹¹¹ We may also contrast this wealth of evidence to the relative lack of such evidence from Egypt. The Pachomian foundation at

---

101 *Chronicon Paschale* 360.
102 For a detailed treatment of Basil's facility see Crislip, *From monastery to hospital*, 103–120.
103 Sozomen *Hist. Eccl.* 6.34.
104 *Or.* 43.63.
105 *Ep.* 94.
106 *Ep.* 150.
107 Epiphanius, *Pan.* 75.3.7. This is certainly more likely than the suggestion of Barrett-Lennard, "Canons of Hippolytus", 163–164, that Basil had taken the idea from Egypt.
108 Horden, "Poverty", 722.
109 Horden, "Poverty", 723.
110 *Ep.* 22.
111 Sozomen *Hist. Eccl.* 3.16.12–16.

Tabbenesi may have had a place for "sick brothers",[112] but as Horden points out,[113] this is not a general refuge for the poor. We may see this as an internal function of a Pachomian monastery, akin to slave hospitals in great estates. The evidence for the foundation of hospices and hospitals in Egypt indicates that these are much later developments.[114]

As such the provision of a hospice, and the appointment of a steward to care for this resource, points not to Egypt but to an area between Constantinople and Antioch as the place in which this Hippolytean provision was redacted. The direction that the sick should not remain, but only the poor should sleep in the church's property, perhaps as a result answers the question of the extent to which these "hospitals" engaged in medical activities, rather than simply being places of poor relief. That is to say, although health was a concern, it was not the function of this hospice to heal but to offer relief to those impoverished by sickness.[115] The indication that the place of lying-in might be described as "in the church" again indicates a complex around a church like that described by Basil, and indeed in *Test. Dom.* 1.19. This in turn indicates that the community envisaged is not a scattered rural community, but nor is it a major urban centre like Antioch itself, given that *Can. Hipp.* 37 envisages that all the clergy will gather with the bishop on a regular basis.

Once this provenance is recognized then other minor points fall into place. Thus we may readily compare the duties of the widows set out at *Can. Hipp.* 9, "frequent prayer, ministry to the sick, and much fasting" to those set out in *Apostolic church order*

---

112 So Crislip, *From monastery to hospital*, 11, 20.
113 Horden, "Poverty", 720.
114 Horden, "Poverty", 730.
115 It is the relative lack of medical provision found in Eustathian houses that causes Crislip, *From monastery to hospital*, 129–130, to doubt Eustathian influence on Basil. It may be that the hospice of *Canones Hippolyti* is more "Eustathian" than "Basilian."

21, the fact that the episcopal ordination takes place on a sabbath, as it does in *Vit. Pol.* 22, and likewise involves a rite of seating, and indeed the parallel observed above between the language of *Can. Hipp.* 37 and that of Gregory Nazianzen.

We may also observe similarities between the ordination prayer for a deacon in *Can. Hipp.* 5 and that of *Const. ap.* 8.18. Both use Stephen as a model for the diaconate, and both pray that the deacon might minister without blame or guilt. Since this is not the ordination prayer found in *Traditio apostolica* this means either that both have chosen to replace the original with a prayer circulating in their own context, or that the same alteration has been made in the recension of *Traditio apostolica* which is found in their community. In either event a common context is indicated, which common context might well be Antiochene. The prayer in *Canones Hippolyti*, moreover, implies that the rite included a consignation, a ritual known in the ordination of bishops in fourth-century Antioch.[116]

This does not mean that this Asian document might not have received a further revision in an Egyptian context.

As indications of an Egyptian provenance we have noted the prayer to be said at the offering of first-fruits (with parallels in Egyptian liturgy), the common grounds with certain statements in the *Sententiae* of Nicaea (an acknowledged Egyptian document), and the statement that Lent is a fasting period, apparently not distinguishing the paschal fast. It is possible that the approach to purity, particularly in *Can. Hipp.* 18,[117] given the strong parallels with the statements of Dionysius and Timothy of Alexandria, reflects an Egyptian rather than an Asian or Cappadocian con-

---

116 So Bradshaw, *Rites of ordination*, 91–92 with reference to evidence from John Chrysostom.
117 For Achelis, *Ältesten Quellen*, 147, this was a manifest interpolation.

cern.[118] However, we should note that *Test. Dom.* 1.23 precludes a widow who is menstruating from approaching, and similarly bars a bishop who has had a wet dream from celebrating, requiring fasting and a ritual bath; further east, a lively debate and diversity of practice is indicated by the discussion of purity, particularly menstrual purity but one extending to other sources of pollution, in *Didascalia apostolorum.* Chrysostom similarly is exercised by the observance of Jewish customs in Antioch,[119] and so we cannot be sure that these passages are not part of the original reworking of *Traditio apostolica.*

The parallels observed to the *Sententiae* of Nicaea, and those with recognizably Egyptian liturgical provenance are, we may observe, to be found in expansions and additions to the Hippolytean original, rather than in any direct rewriting, although the additions may be prompted by catchwords. The suggestion is thus that a Cappadocian revision of *Traditio apostolica* has been subject to further redaction in an Egyptian context.

We may support such a hypothesis with reference to the first part of *Can. Hipp.* 21: "The presbyters gather every day at the church, as do the deacons, the subdeacons (ὑποδιάκων), the readers (ἀναγνώστης), and all the congregation, at the time when the cock crows. They are to take up prayers, and psalms, and reading of Scripture, and the prayer, in accordance with the direction of the apostle, who said 'Attend to reading until I return.'" Coquin suggests that this pattern is that of a synaxis.[120] Bradshaw agrees, whilst observing that cock-crow is an exceptionally early time for a public synaxis, and that it is unusual to find Scripture read at

---

118 Thus Wendebourg, "Die altestamentlichen Reinheitsgesetze" 166–167, noting *Canones Hippolyti*, suggests that the Jewish presence in Alexandria had brought about Christian observation of purity laws within the Christian communities of the city.
119 See on this, and for references, Wilken, *John Chrysostom.*
120 Coquin, *Canons,* 119.

such a synaxis.¹²¹ He notes, however, that the time and the reading of Scripture is mirrored in what is said of Egyptian monastic practice in the *Institutes* of Cassian (on Scripture, *Inst.* 2.5, on the time, *Inst.* 3.5.) What is most interesting is that the institution of prayer at cockcrow and the reading of Scripture are both said to have been relatively recent introductions native to Egypt. This would indicate that this canon, which is without parallel in *Traditio apostolica*, is a specifically Egyptian interpolation undertaken towards the end of the redactional process. In further support of this we may observe, with Chase,¹²² the fact that all of this is paralleled in *Sent. Conc. Nic.* 2.1–4. Whether the further reference to prayer at cock-crow at *Can. Hipp.* 27 is also from this level of revision is less clear; we may note that the emphasis on nocturnal prayer in this Canon shares a pre-occupation with ps-Athanasius *Virg.* 20, with Basil *Reg. Fus.* 37, and with *Testamentum Domini* which refers to this at 1.22, 1.32, 1.42, and 2.24 and in which, in 2.19, the ascetics extend the paschal vigil until dawn. We may also note similarities between the *horarium* of *Can. Hipp.* 25 and *Test. Dom.* 2.24; this triplication of statements regarding times of prayer indicates that one at least is a later addition to the text.

The period of such revision, given the relatively simple pneumatology of the preface, as compared to the statement of co-equality in the baptismal liturgy, as well as the common ground with the *Canonical responses* of Timothy, might be the 370s or, in view of Cassian's statement that the innovations in the office were relatively recent, slightly later. The original Asian revision of *Traditio apostolica*, on which this Egyptian recension was based, might not have been substantially earlier, as the indications are that it is to be attributed to the 340s–360s.

---

121 Bradshaw, *Canons*, 26. The evidence for such synaxes is gathered at Bradshaw, *Daily prayer*, 72–92.
122 Chase, "Another look", 11.

## 6 The liturgies of Canones Hippolyti

It is unfortunate that we cannot be sure at many points of what is derived from the original Asian or Antiochene reworking of *Traditio apostolica*, and what might have resulted from subsequent, probably Egyptian, revision, although the suggestion that the *horarium* of *Can. Hipp.* 25 is original is canvassed above. Moreover, when *Canones Hippolyti* follows *Traditio apostolica* we cannot assume that this was local practice. Thus deductions regarding liturgical practice can only be made when the *Canones* depart from their Hippolytean model. Nonetheless there are some potential insights into liturgical history available from the document. In particular, if there is a basis for the case presented that *Canones Hippolyti* is indeed not Egyptian, then much supposed evidence for Egyptian liturgy in the fourth century suddenly disappears. Although this may seem a negative result, it means that the study of Egyptian liturgy in the fourth century will not be relying on a source erroneously given such a provenance.

### 6.1 The ordination rites

The ordination rites of *Canones Hippolyti* are clearly derived from those of *Traditio apostolica*, and thus where they follow the source we cannot have any certainty that they mirror practice in the *Canones Hippolyti* community. Where they depart, however, they may give some indication of local practice. Thus the ordination prayer for a bishop is modelled on that of *Traditio apostolica*, but there is an interesting variation in the rubrics, already noted at 5 above, where the provision of *Traditio apostolica* is rewritten so that rather than "one of the bishops" undertaking the handlaying it is undertaken by "one of the bishops and presbyters."[123] We may suggest that a redactor familiar with presbyteral ordination of the *episkopos*, faced with a text enforcing episcopal ordina-

---

123  *Canones Hippolyti* 2.

tion of the *episkopos*, expanded the text in order to embrace the continued involvement of the presbyterate. In the past, assuming the Egyptian provenance of *Canones Hippolyti*, I suggested that this alteration came about due to the manner in which Egyptian bishops came to be ordained by the bishop of Alexandria.[124] In response to Müller, who suggested that the handlaying by the presbyter was the original reading, and asked whether a redactor in the fourth century would make the addition of a presbyter,[125] I responded that in an Egyptian backwater in the fourth century he might well. The same, however, is true of a Cappadocian backwater. *Apostolic church order*, whilst saying nothing of ordination, is clear that episcopal appointment is undertaken by a group of twelve men who form what we may recognize as a local presbytery.[126] It is this which is reflected in *Canones Hippolyti*. It is also noteworthy that the ordination rite does not mention the rite of seating, even though the chair is a mark of episcopal office in this community. This absence is the result of following *Traditio apostolica*.

A similar equation of presbyter and bishop emerges from *Can. Hipp.* 4, where the presbyteral ordination prayer from *Traditio apostolica* is omitted. Rather than reflecting a primitive presbyteral order, however, this represents a situation in which the original Asian presbyteral patrons have developed into an ascetic group, led by a bishop, as they have in the communities behind *Apostolic Church Order* and *Testamentum Domini*. The bishop is thus one among the presbyters, as the leading male ascetic of the group. Nonetheless ordination is now the preserve of bishops, leading to the clarification in *Can. Hipp.* 4 that a presbyter does not have the power of ordination.[127]

---

124 Stewart, *Original bishops*, 343–344.
125 Müller, "Kleine Beiträge", 228.
126 Apostolic church order 16.
127 This provision puzzles Riedel, *Kirchenrechtsquellen*, 203, n. 2, who asks: "Wie stimmt dazu der letzte Satz von Canon 2?".

As already noted, the episcopal ordination prayer in *Can. Hipp.* 3 follows *Trad. ap.* 3; there are, however, some interesting alterations. Omitting the Old Testament typology the prayer asks that the bishop be given the grace of healing. Most interesting, however, among the ordination prayers, is the diaconal ordination prayer of *Can. Hipp.* 5. As already noted, this has a strong similarity to that found in *Const. ap.* 8.18. Given that *Constitutiones apostolorum* is rather fuller than *Canones Hippolyti* we may suggest that both were drawing on the same local euchological tradition, and that *Canones Hippolyti* represents a more primitive version of the prayer. With regard to the rite, moreover, we may again note Bradshaw's suggestion that the phrase within the prayer "that he may triumph over the powers of the evil one through the sign of your cross with which you mark him" indicates a consignation as part of the ordination rite,[128] observing with him the evidence for such a rite in fourth-century Antioch, referring to Chrysostom *Hom. in Matt.* 54.7 in which ordination is mentioned in a catalogue of liturgical occasions at which consignation is employed.

## 6.2 The baptismal rites

The baptismal rites of *Canones Hippolyti* are clearly indebted to *Traditio apostolica*, though traces of a distinct rite show through.

### 6.2.1 The prebaptismal rites

The first point to observe is the insertion of an *apotaxis* and a *syntaxis* prior to the acquiescent baptismal creed. I have argued at length elsewhere that the apotactic and syntactic form is the most ancient form of baptismal affirmation in Asia and Syria, and that this might have a trinitarian or a christological shape.[129]

---

128  Bradshaw, *Canons*, 14.
129  Stewart, "The early Alexandrian baptismal creed", 237–253 and refs.

Thus the trinitarian confession found as a syntaxis in *Canones Hippolyti* may reasonably be ascribed to the redactor, as a reflection of the baptismal rite native to this community, which has been uncomfortably combined with the rite of *Traditio apostolica*. Such a trinitarian form of the *syntaxis* may be found in the Cyrilline *Catecheses mystagogicae:* τότε σοι ἐγένετο εἰπεῖν Πιστεύω εἰς τὸν πατέρα καὶ τὸν υἱὸν καὶ εἰς τὸ ἅγιον πνεῦμα καὶ εἰς βάπτισμα μετανοίας,[130] as in the Syriac *Historia Johannis*, in which baptismal candidates variously confess "I believe in the name of the Father and the Son and the Spirit of holiness"[131] and "We believe in the name of the Father and the Son and the Spirit of holiness and we will never know anything else."[132] Typically of Asian and west Syrian rites in the fourth century, the baptismal profession is a *syntaxis* following on from the *apotaxis*, and followed immediately by baptism.

### 6.2.2 The baptismal "formula"

A particular sign of the redactor's discomfort in combining the responsive rite with which he is familiar with the acquiescent form of *Traditio apostolica* is the concluding rubric: "And each time he says 'I baptize you in the name of the Father, and of the Son, and of the Holy Spirit, the equal Trinity.'"

The redactor is clearly confused by the direction that the candidate be baptized three times in an acquiescent form without the baptizer speaking any formula,[133] and so introduces a baptismal formula at the end of the acquiescent baptismal form, apparently to be repeated three times. As such this is not a "realistic" rite, but an attempt to combine the form in *Traditio apostolica*,

---

130 Cyril of Jerusalem *Cat. myst.* 1.9.
131 *Historia Johannis* 22. *Historia Johannis* is a late fourth-century work of Syrian origin. Edition to which reference is made is Lollar, *History of John*.
132 *Hist. Johannis* 30.
133 I prefer the term "acquiescent" to the more common "interrogatory." For the reasons see my "Early Alexandrian baptismal creed".

which is acquiescent, with the responsive form with which he is familiar.[134] This implies that a baptismal formula "I baptize..." was in use in this community, though used to accompany a responsive rite, rather than to follow an acquiescent rite, and so said only once.

Although this formula is echoed in statements of Basil,[135] we cannot proceed from Basil's allusions to a statement of the formula employed by the baptizer. There has been no systematic exploration of the history of the baptismal formula since Whitaker's effort in 1965.[136] This treatment needs radical revision, not least due to the weight put by Whitaker on the evidence of the *Acta* of Xanthike and Polyxena in which Paul baptizes stating: "We baptize you in the name of the Father and of the Son and of the Holy Spirit" and where Andrew is likewise said to baptize in the name of the Trinity. Whereas Whitaker sees this as evidence for the use of a first-person formula in the third century,[137] this is problematic. For whereas these *Acta* were dated by James to the third century, a dating to which Whitaker was indebted, more recent consideration has demonstrated that they are the product of the fifth century.[138] As such they cannot stand the evidential weight that Whitaker wishes to put upon them. Nonetheless, in any revised history of the baptismal formula *Canones Hippolyti* provides vital evidence for its use in the fourth century in the active form. Whitaker had suggested that such an active form was in use in Syria since from the work of Chrysostom we are able to reconstruct the formula "N is baptized in the name of the Father and of the Son and of the Holy Spirit" on which

---

134 For Hanssens, "Édition critique", 541, this peculiar rubric is seen as reason to deny a fourth-century date to *Canones Hippolyti*, because it does not conform to what is known of Egyptian baptismal rites in the period. It is, however, not a reflection of a real rite but a redactional construction.
135 *Ep.* 159.2; *De Sancto Spirito* 10.24; 12.28.
136 Whitaker, "History", 1–12.
137 Whitaker, "History", 5.
138 So Klauck, *Apocryphal acts*, 251.

Chrysostom comments: "He does not say 'I baptize N' but 'N is baptized.'" Not long thereafter we find reference to the same formula employed by the baptizer in the work of Theodore of Mopsuestia and in that of Narsai. Thus Whitaker deduces from Chrysostom's comments a somewhat defensive tone, and suggests that the authors are trying to distance themselves from another formula in use, in which the baptizer states "I baptize".[139] Although the evidence on which he based this assertion of the existence of such a formula is now wanting, *Canones Hippolyti* tends to support such a view and fill the evidential gap. Such would fit, moreover, with the pattern of interrogation known in the Antiochene and Asian baptismal rites in which a confession is elicited from the candidate before entering the water.

It might also be noted that the same is true of the Egyptian baptismal rite, though evidence for the pronunciation of any formula from the fourth century is wanting.[140] As such, this final rubric leaves with something of a puzzle; whereas it may speak of an active formula in use in the original community producing *Canones Hippolyti*, it is also possible that this too is a later addition by the Egyptian editor.[141] The state of the evidence is such

---

139  Whitaker, "History", 5.
140  There is, however, some later evidence. In the *Erotapokrisis Cyrilli et Stephani*, an anonymous dialogue preserved in Coptic between two deacons and Cyril of Alexandria, a tale is told of a mother who was unsure which of her two sons had been baptized. Cyril directs that they should both be baptized conditionally with the active formula: "Him who has not been baptized, him I baptize in the name of the Father, and of the Son, and of the Holy Spirit." (Text in Crum, *Der Papyruscodex saec. VI-VII der Phillippsbibliothek in Cheltenham*, 46; translation, 104).) We might also refer to the Timothy of Alexandria *Resp. can.* 38, on the subject of conditional baptism. To the question regarding the form, Timothy responds that the baptizer should say: "If you are not baptized, I baptize you in the name of the Father, and of the Son, and of the Holy Spirit." (Text in Pitra, *Iuris ecclesiastici Graecorum historia et monumenta*, 638.) However, this text may well be late and pseudonymous (so Psarev, "19th Canonical Answer", 305.)
141  Such is the suggestion of Kretschmar, "Beiträge zur Geschichte der Liturgie", 39. Kretschmar would see this addition as rather later, in my opinion unnecessarily.

that the presence of this formula cannot be used to ascertain its Asian origin, but likewise it cannot be used to deny it.[142]

### 6.2.3 The baptismal creed

Although the acquiescent creed has been transplanted from *Traditio apostolica* into *Canones Hippolyti*, it is not without its own peculiarities. First, however, we should note that this tends to provide further evidence that *Canones Hippolyti* is not Egyptian, at least not at the main level of redaction. The modern Coptic rite includes a five-membered creed, which is very close in form to the credal fragment found in the (fourth century, Egyptian) Deir Balyzeh papyrus: "I believe in God, Father Almighty and in his only begotten Son Our Lord Jesus Christ and in the Holy Spirit and in resurrection of the flesh in the holy catholic church" (although the baptismal context of the fragment here is far from clear.)[143] It is also very close to the first credal question in the Sahidic version of the baptismal rite in *Traditio apostolica:* once clearly post-Nicene material such as the *homoousion* has been removed we may see that the candidate is enjoined to say: "I believe in the only true God, the Father the Almighty, and his only begotten Son Jesus Christ our Lord, our Saviour with his Holy Spirit, in the holy catholic apostolic church and in eternal life."[144] Again, the five-fold pattern is apparent. We may also note the letter of Alexander of Alexandria to Alexander of Constantinople,[145] in which, towards the conclusion of the letter Alexander proclaims his own faith, which he claims as that

---

142 As does Brakmann, "Alexandreia und die Kanones des Hippolyt", 140 n. 10, responding to Kretschmar's suggestion that the *Canones* might be Asian. Brakmann suggests that there is nothing specifically Asian about this baptismal rite. We have to ask, therefore, where he thinks the *syntaxis* has come from, if it is not a rite originating in Asia.
143 So Stewart, *Two early Egyptian liturgical papyri*, 17–21.
144 Till & Leipoldt, *Der koptische Text der Kirchenordnung Hippolyts*, 20–21. The Ethiopic and Arabic versions, dependent on Coptic, are similar.
145 Apud Theodoret *Hist. Eccl.* 1.4.

of the apostolic church, a confession which, as Lanne shows, may be grouped under the same five headings, namely belief in each of the three persons of the Godhead, the church, and the resurrection.[146] Thus, were *Canones Hippolyti* Egyptian, we might reasonably expect to find this five-membered creed, rather than that which is found. However, the confession of the church, and the resurrection, which appear in *Traditio apostolica* (on the basis of both Latin and Aksumite Ethiopic) is actually omitted from *Canones Hippolyti*.

The third article of the creed, whilst not Egyptian, is in any event puzzling. the baptismal candidate is asked: "Do you believe in the Holy Spirit, the paraklete, who flows forth from the Father and the Son?" "Flows forth" here renders *fāʿ ḍa*, which, Coquin suggests, renders Coptic ⲡⲱϩⲧ or ⲡⲱⲛ, which in turn renders ἐκχέεσθαι or ἐκχέειν.[147] The word "from" (*min*) might, he suggests, also be the agent of a passive, thus ἐκχυνόμενον. It is hard to parallel such a statement from the fourth century, though such a statement is found attributed by Gelasius Cyzicus to Leontius of Caesarea:[148] καὶ τὸ πνεῦμα τὸ ἅγιον, ὅτι ἐξ αὐτοῦ λαμβάνομεν ἅπαντες οἱ πιστοί, τῆς αὐτῆς ὂν οὐσίας ἧς ὁ πατὴρ καὶ ὁ υἱός, ἐκπορευόμενον μὲν ἐκ τοῦ πατρὸς ἴδιον δὲ ὂν τοῦ υἱοῦ, καθάπερ ἀνωτέρω ἀπεδείξαμεν, ὅτι δὲ ἐξ αὐτοῦ (the Son) ἡμῖν ἀναβλύζον... *fāʿḍa* might readily be rendered by ἀναβλύζω, though Lim supplies ample reasons for seeing the dialogue in the context of which this statement is set, and therefore its contents, as suspect;[149] moreover the theological language used throughout this dialogue is typical of a period much later in the fourth century. Nonetheless, stripped of the *homoousion* this statement is comparable to that of the *Canones*, and one wonders whether there is

---

146 Lanne, "La confession", 221.
147 Botte, "Origines", 58, similarly suggests ἐκχυνόμενον.
148 *Syntagma* 2.23.5.
149 Lim, *Public disputation*, 209–213.

some echo of an authentically Caesarean formula here, which Gelasius has expanded in an ultra-Nicene direction. There is certainly nothing in the version of the *Canones* which is unthinkable in fourth-century homoian circles.

We may, moreover, suggest that the creed is not speaking of the eternal generation of the Spirit, but of the experience of the Spirit in the church.[150] This description of the work of the Spirit, together with the use of the term "paraklete", is found in a number of fourth-century conciliar creeds.[151] Among them we may note the fourth creed of Antioch (341), the *makrostichos* creed (Antioch, 345), the third creed of Sirmium (357, the "blasphemy"), the fourth creed of Sirmium (359, the "dated creed"), the Thracian-Nicene creed (359), the ninth confession of Seleucia (359), the homoian creed of Constantinople (360).

Whatever the questions this article poses, this reworking of *Traditio apostolica*, alongside the addition of the words "co-equal Trinity" to the Trinitarian statement of the baptismal formula, provide indications that liturgical rites were being employed to convey doctrine, and that the clarification of trinitarian doctrine was a fundamental concern of the redactor. This in turn indicates that these expansions of the baptismal ritual come from the same hand which produced the preface.

### 6.2.4 The post-baptismal ceremonies

We should also observe that the redactor of *Canones Hippolyti* has introduced alterations to the post-baptismal ceremonies of *Traditio apostolica*. Thus whereas *Traditio apostolica* simply states that a presbyter anoints the newly baptized, in the *Canones* the candidate is anointed after baptism on *his* forehead, mouth, and breast. Bradshaw compares this to the procedure of anointing the

---

150 So Riedel, *Kirchenrechtsquellen*, 212, on the basis of the possible range of meanings in *fāl ḍa* in its various forms.
151 As noted by Botte, "Origines", 57.

forehead, ears, nose, and breast in the *Catecheses mystagogicae*,[152] and this leads him to ask where this is an example of Egyptian influence on the Jerusalem liturgy, referring to Cuming's suggestions that there had been such a line of influence.[153] We may respond that this assumes an Egyptian provenance for *Canones Hippolyti*, though it is fair to point out that Antiochene rites lack any corresponding anointing, and thus this development of the original presents something of a conundrum. Apart from *Catecheses mystagogicae* we may note the seventh canon of the Council of Constantinople, which regulates the reception of baptized heretics through sealing them with oil on the forehead, eyes, nostrils, mouth, and ears. This canon, however, is spurious; since the seventeenth century it has been recognized as an extract from a letter of the church of Constantinople to Martyrius of Antioch, dating from the middle of the fifth century.[154] Nonetheless it may give some indication of the nature of post-baptismal anointing at the period of its composition. How this related post-baptismal anointing appears in the fourth-century *Canons of Hippolytus*, and indeed in *Catecheses mystagogicae* (on the assumption that they derive from the fourth century)[155] remains a mystery. We may reasonably state, however, that such a procedure was known in the fourth century, whilst having no insight to offer on the place of its origin or its prior history.

We may also note that whereas we can be confident in reconstructing the procedure of *Traditio apostolica* as presbyteral anointing, followed by episcopal handlaying, episcopal anointing, and then an episcopal consignation, the *Canones* have combined the final anointing with the consignation, by omitting the prayer said at the episcopal anointing, and thus having the bishop

---

152 Bradshaw, *Canons*, 23 with reference to *Cat. Myst.* 3.4.
153 Cuming, "Egyptian elements", 117–124; Cuming deals with the post-baptismal anointing at p.123.
154 The insight of Beveridge, ΣΥΝΟΔΙΚΟΝ, II, annotationes, 98–102.
155 The most recent discussion is that of Johnson, *St Cyril of Jerusalem*, 37–55.

anoint the candidate as a consignation.[156] It is probable that the redactor, like Theodore of Mopsuestia, knew of a consignation but no other post-baptismal anointing,[157] and that this has brought about the combination of the two acts of the original into one. It is not clear that Theodore's consignation included anointing;[158] the witness of *Const. ap.* 3.16 may combine with that of the *Canones* here to answer that in the affirmative.

Finally we may note Bradshaw's comment on the post-baptismal anointing prayer that insofar as it diverts from that found at *Trad. ap.* 21.21, it may represent some local tradition.[159] He observes, nonetheless, that it is distinct from those prayers found in Sarapion *Sacr.* 11 and in the modern Coptic rite. As such we may consider it possible that it reflects Asian practice.

### 6.2.5 Conclusion

Beyond tending to indicate that oil was used in post-baptismal consignation in Syria, this study of the baptismal rites of *Canones Hippolyti* does not convey any new information, but tends to support what has already been hypothesized, thus strengthening certainty about the conclusions that have already been reached by extending the evidential base on which we may understand baptismal practices in west Syria and Asia in the fourth century. However, at the same time it raises new questions regarding the use of a baptismal formula, the strange version of the creed which it employs, and the practice of post-baptismal anointing of those organs which, in western rites, were anointed prior to baptism.

---

156  See the note at the translation ad loc. on the disputed question of the text here.
157  Cat. Myst. 14.27.
158  See the discussion in Yarnold, *The awe-inspiring rites of initiation*, 198, n. 65.
159  Bradshaw, *Canons*, 24.

## 6.3 The Pascha of Canones Hippolyti

As we have seen, the paschal fast of *Canones Hippolyti*, as well as its method of calculation, are Quartodeciman in character. These are in keeping with their probably Asian origin. As such the statement in *Can. Hipp.* 22 that "not even a word should be spoken with joy during it, but with sadness, knowing that the Lord of all, who is impassible, suffered on our behalf", lends support to the hypothesis that one reason given in Quartodeciman circles for the paschal fast was that of participation in the sufferings of Jesus. We may also observe with interest the statement in *Can. Hipp.* 38 that nobody is to sleep or rest at the Paschal vigil, but should be vigilant. This may be read in the light of *Test. Dom.* 2.19 that not even infants are allowed to sleep, and that deacons and readers are to ensure that all are awake. This, Strobel suggests, reflects the eschatological nature of the Quartodeciman Pascha, in keeping with traditions formed within second Temple Judaism.[160] Thus although no liturgical details are given it is notable that the only liturgy to which any reference would appear to be made is that of the vigil; there is no mention of an Easter morning gathering. This is, once again, in keeping with the process of liturgical development in mid-fourth century Cappadocia.[161] It may also be noted that there is no indication that anything akin to the triduum has developed at the time of the *Canones*. The same remains true in Cappadocia late into the fourth-century.[162]

Again, this tells us little that we did not already suspect, but confirms our suspicion, and lends colour to our understanding of the nature of the Quartodeciman paschal vigil.

---

160 Strobel, *Ursprung und Geschichte*, 39.
161 See Buchinger, "Breaking the fast", 199–201.
162 Noted by Buchinger, "Easter cycle", 45–77.

## 6.4 Eucharistic and other ritual meals

Whereas the account of the episcopal ordination omits the eucharistic prayer to be said by the bishop in *Traditio apostolica*, there is reference elsewhere to ritual meals. In *Can. Hipp.* 19 an account, largely indebted to *Traditio apostolica*, is given of the baptismal Eucharist, in *Can. Hipp.* 29 material originating in *Traditio apostolica* is thoroughly rewritten to concern care of the altar, and of the eucharistic species, and *Can. Hipp.* 23–35 recast material deriving from *Traditio apostolica*.

*Can. Hipp.* 29 is interesting in that it refers to the veiling of the altar,[163] but the *Canones* give little information about eucharistic meals. There may be some indirect evidence in *Can. Hipp.* 33, regarding funeral entertainments. The canon, in stating that the participants should receive exorcized bread before they sit, that a catechumen should not be present at the Lord's Supper, that the participants should eat and drink only to sufficiency and not get drunk, that they do so quietly and to the praise of God, is presenting us with a garbled version of various provisions in *Traditio apostolica*, namely *Trad. ap.* 28.5b ("in the same way let a catechumen receive the same, though exorcized"), *Trad. ap.* 27.1, ("a catechumen shall not sit at the Lord's Supper"), *Trad. ap.* 28.1, 3 ("when you eat and drink, do so with integrity and do not get drunk... And if you are invited to eat, eat so that you have had <just> enough"), and *Trad. ap.* 32.3 ("and in all things which are eaten they shall give thanks to the holy God, eating to his glory"). We may reasonably suggest that they are incorporated solely to use and retain the source text, much of which is no longer applicable or comprehensible. But the setting for these instructions, stating that should there be a funeral entertainment it should not be on a Sunday and should be preceded by the Eucharist, is without parallel in *Traditio apostolica* and is thus probably reflective

---

163 So also *Test. Dom.* 1.19, 1.23.

of the community which produced this instruction.

*Can. Hipp.* 33 provides that the Eucharist should be celebrated before the *analempsis*, but this could well be the regulation of an earlier custom in which a eucharistic meal of a particular funereal type was celebrated. Sadly we have no details of what such a meal might entail, but this provision does provide evidence of a funeral or memorial meal in (we may now say) Christian Asian circles, and the fourth-century regulation of such activities through the instruction that a normative Eucharist should begin the proceedings. As such it should not take place on a Sunday in order not to displace the regular Sunday Eucharist. It is quite possible that the original rite incorporated a eucharistic meal of a non-normative type, which is being replaced by a Eucharist, followed by an agapic event as a remainder of the more primitive ritual, which had been a eucharistic meal as part of a *Sättigungsmahl*.

*Can. Hipp.* 32 reads: "If there is a meal (*wal'ima*) or a supper ('*aṣā*') which somebody gives for the poor and it is κυριακόν (the term is transliterated), when the bishop is present..." What follows is a recension of the opening of *Trad. ap.* 25, with the prayer over the lamp. The introduction, however, is clearly redactional. Coquin translates the first word "*wal'ima*" as "*agapē*."[164] This is possible, but we should note that there is no certain evidence. What the passage does, however, indicate, is the possibility that a meal for the poor might be given by a patron.

Historically there has been a degree of confusion regarding this canon, both in the statement that the meal might be κυριακόν and in the statement following that the "thanksgiving" should precede the meal. In the notes to the translation the position is taken that the phrase means that the meal is in the church, a practice known and outlawed in the canons of Laodicea, and that

---

164 As does Haneberg, *Canones*, 91, though Riedel, *Kirchenrechtsquellen*, 221, rejects this rendering.

the thanksgiving (the term εὐχαριστία is transliterated) simply refers to an opening grace.¹⁶⁵ Whatever the obscurities of this passage, that the redactor has constructed such an introduction to a passage which otherwise would seem hard to understand is an indication that in this community at least entertainments might be given to the poor. We cannot, however, know the extent to which these were liturgical events, but may be assured that they were not eucharistic. Achelis, Lietzmann and Hamman, however, have each reconstructed a liturgy from this and the following canons.¹⁶⁶ Lietzmann's reconstruction is of particular significance because, having taken the reference to a εὐχαριστία at the beginning of the liturgy (*quddās*, a word which may refer to the entire eucharistic liturgy) as a reference to the Eucharist as such, he draws a line of development from here back to the *Didache* as representing one of his two types of original Eucharist, seeing both as a pattern of Eucharist followed by agape.¹⁶⁷

Given that much of this is derived from *Traditio apostolica*, I would be wary of reaching too many conclusions based on this evidence. It is possible that some of this material is retained and rewritten due to the extent to which it coheres with known local practice, for instance the second part of *Can. Hipp.* 35, regarding supper for widows, whilst dependent on *Traditio apostolica*, may have been retained because it is applicable to the situation of the redactor,¹⁶⁸ but beyond stating that the *Canones* imply that the practice of giving charity meals in churches, which might be known as *agapai*, was known, an insight which coheres with other Asian evidence, it would be unwise to go much further. As

---

165 The same conclusion is suggested by Batiffol, *Études d'histoire et de théologie*, 321–323.
166 Achelis, *Ältesten Quellen*, 202–205; Lietzmann, *Messe und Herrenmahl*, 199–200; Hamman, *Vie liturgique*, 191–192.
167 Lietzmann, *Messe und Herrenmahl*, 233.
168 We should also note the appearance of comparable material in *Didasc. ap.* 2.28.1.

observed in the notes to the translation, it is unlikely, as some have asserted, that the Eucharist is celebrated at the beginning of this rite.

## 6.5 Healing rituals

It has been argued that there is a particular concern within *Canones Hippolyti* for sickness and health.[169] Many of the instances, however, are carried over from *Traditio apostolica*, though there are some occasions where the original is expanded in an interesting direction. Thus there is a significant addition to the episcopal ordination prayer asking that the candidate be given the authority "to release every bond of demonic oppression, to heal the sick, and to trample the devil swiftly under his feet". It is also possible to exaggerate this concern through seeing the hospice as primarily a hospital for the sick, rather than a hospice for the impoverished. The steward cares for those in the hospice who are sick, as in *Can. Athan.* 49, but this is simply an extension of his concern for the inmates. As noted already, the provision regarding the clay pots is entirely a reworking of a provision in *Trad. ap.* 40 regarding clay tiles to seal *loculi*, though the suggestion that these are the stores of provisions[170] is reasonable.

However, the concern is real, even if capable of overstatement. Thus whereas the provision that those who are sick and have homes are not to remain in the church overnight[171] may be intended to prevent the better-off taking advantage of the provision for the destitute made in the church's hospice, it may also be intended to dissuade the sick from practising incubation.[172] The provision of oil and water for the sick found in *Can. Hipp.* 21 is known elsewhere both in Egypt, as the *Sacramentary* of Sarapion

---

169  Note in particular Barrett-Lennard, "Canons of Hippolytus" on this and as a reference point throughout this section.
170  Barrett-Lennard, "Canons of Hippolytus", 159.
171  *Can. Hipp.* 24.
172  So Barrett-Lennard, "Canons of Hippolytus", 161–162.

has a prayer for the oil and water of the sick,[173] and a further prayer over "oil for the sick, or for bread, or for water" (though in the prayer only oil is mentioned),[174] and in Antioch, as *Const. ap.* 8.29 has a prayer over oil and water which is clearly intended to heal and to restore health. Since the evidence that can be provided with a provenance is both Egyptian (Sarapion) and Antiochene (*Constitutiones apostolorum*), the origin of the *Canones Athanasii* being uncertain, we cannot say that there is a particular Egyptian concern for sickness and healing expressed in *Canones Hippolyti*.[175] We may, however, agree that through these provisions we are brought to appreciate the *realia* of the daily lives of these early Christians.

## 7. Conclusion

We thus conclude that whereas *Canones Hippolyti* are, as previously argued, a product of the middle of the fourth century, they have been expanded at a slightly later stage. More significantly, whereas they have previously been assumed to have derived from an Egyptian provenance, a Cappadocian or Antiochene provenance for the *Hauptwerk* is far more probable, although it is likely that the later expansion is Egyptian.

Quite apart from the implications for the study of the liturgy enshrined in *Canones Hippolyti*, and the social setting which they presuppose, this conclusion has implications for the study of the transmission of *Traditio apostolica*, and for the generation of reworked church orders generally. It is particularly intriguing that Cappadocian churches should produce *Apostolic Church Order* (a reworking of earlier church order material) and *Testamentum Domini* (a combination of *Traditio apostolica* with a native ascetic

---

173 Sarapion *Sacr.* 5.
174 Sarapion *Sacr.* 17.
175 So Barrett-Lennard, "Canons of Hippolytus", in conclusion.

rule which may reasonably be termed a church order) within a few years of each other, and that around the same time *Traditio apostolica* should again be independently reworked to produce *Canones Hippolyti*, either in the same Cappadocian region, or perhaps slightly to the south east towards Antioch. What is even more remarkable is that within a few years, again in Antioch, we should have the production of *Constitutiones apostolorum*, again reworking *Traditio apostolica* as part of the eighth book, as well as incorporating a reworked *Didascalia* and a reworked *Didache*. Finally we should note a further intriguing aspect of this phenomenon, namely that *Apostolic church order*, *Constitutiones apostolorum*, and *Canones Hippolyti*, each produced within a relatively short period and in the same area, should each, independently, set their church order material as material deriving from a fictive council, an apostolic council in the case of *Apostolic church order* and *Constitutiones apostolorum*, and in the case of *Canones Hippolyti* either the council of Nicaea or another of the councils of the mid-fourth century.[176]

I cannot speculate on the rationale behind these reworkings, but suggest that this hardly seems co-incidental. We may also note that *Traditio apostolica* would appear to have been being received in these regions at about this time, as a document in itself rather than as part of a collection,[177] and being received as in some sense an authoritative document, such that its provisions are reworked and recombined with local material, for reasons on which we can only speculate. Once again, new discovery has simply opened up new questions.

---

176 That the division into canons extends at least back to the Greek version of the *Canons* is demonstrated by Coquin, *Canons*, 34–35, in response to the suggestion of Riedel, *Kirchenrechtsquellen*, 200. However, although there is no doubt that the division is ancient, we cannot say it is not a result of the second, possibly Egyptian, recension.

177 Contra Coquin, *Canons*, 40–41, who thought that the document was already circulating as part of a collection.

# Arabic Text and English Translation

Sigla:
The notes to the translation observe the most significant variants, employing a simplified version of the sigla of Coquin.

    d: The Nomocanon of Michael of Damietta
    m: The collection of ps-Macarius
    R: The Berlin canonical collection

Note is not taken of the individual MSS of the distinct witnesses.

The contents list is found in R; there is also a version in Ibn Kabar *Miṣbāḥ al-ẓulma,* shown as K in the apparatus.

For further information on these witnesses see the introduction in the first instance.

References to the works of Achelis, Bradshaw, Coquin, Haneberg, and Riedel without page references are references to their editions and translations ad loc.

بسم الاب والابن والروح القدس الاله الواحد.

القوانين التي وضعها ابوليدس مقدم اساقفة رومية كاوامر الرسل من جهة سيدنا يسوع المسيح. وعدتها ثمانية وثلاثون قانونا.

الاول. لاجل الامانة المقدسة.

الثاني. لاجل الاساقفة.

الثالث. الصلاة على من ترتب اسقفا وترتيب القداس.

الرابع. لاجل قسمة القسيس.

الخامس. لاجل قسمة الشماس.

السادس. لاجل الذين يعاقبون على الامانة.

السابع. لاجل اصطفاء الاغنستسيين والابودياقيين.

الثامن. لاجل مواهب الشفاء.

التاسع. لاجل قسيس يسكن في موضع ليس له ولاجل كرامة الارامل.

العاشر. لاجل الذين يصيرون نصارى.

الحادي عشر. لاجل من يعمل الاصنام والاوثان صائغا كان او مصورا.

الثاني عشر. النهي عن عدة افعال لا يقبل فاعلها الا بعد التوبة.

الثالث عشر. لاجل سلطان او جندي بان لا يقتلوا جملة ولو أُمروا ولا يلبسوا تيجانا ومن له كرامة ولا يفعل العدل الذي في الانجيل يفرق ولا يصلي مع الاسقف.

In the name of the Father and of the Son and of the Holy Spirit, one God.

The canons which Hippolytus, archbishop of Rome,[1] laid down as commandments of the apostles. Their number is thirty-eight canons.[2]

The first: concerning the holy faith.

The second: concerning the bishops.

The third: the prayer upon the one ordered bishop and the ordering of the liturgy.

The fourth: concerning the ordination of the presbyter.

The fifth: concerning the ordination of the deacon.

The sixth: concerning those who are punished for the faith.

The seventh: concerning the selection of the reader (ἀναγνώστης) and the subdeacon (ὑποδιάκων).

The eighth: concerning gifts of healing.

The ninth: concerning a presbyter who dwells in a place not his own, and concerning the honour due to widows.[3]

The tenth: concerning those who become Christians.

The eleventh: concerning those who make idols or images, whether they be jewellers[4] or painters

The twelfth: the prohibition of several acts, and that whoever does them will not be accepted without repentance.

The thirteenth: concerning a magistrate or a soldier, that they are not to kill at all, even if they are ordered; and they are not to wear crowns; and anyone who has an honour, and does not perform the uprightness which is of the Gospel is to be separated, and is not to pray with the bishop.

---

1  Botte,"Origine", 62, suggests that this title "archbishop", given to Hippolytus, assures of the antiquity of the title overall, since this was the regular usage until later in the fourth century, when the title "patriarch" took over. Hanssens, "Édition critique", 541, is less sure.

2  Whereas Riedel, 200, reckoned this list of contents secondary, and the work of the Arabic translator, Coquin, 34-35, demonstrates that it was composed in Greek. If not original, it is nonetheless ancient, and composed, moreover, as Coquin shows, by a scribe with access to *Traditio apostolica*.

3  See the annotation at the chapter heading ad loc.

4  The two Arabic words ṣā'iġ ("jeweller" or "goldsmith") and ṣāniʿ (craftsman) are very similar in appearance. R here has "jeweller" whereas the other witnesses have "craftsman." Similar confusion arises in the canon itself.

الرابع عشر. لا يصر نصراني جنديا.

الخامس عشر. عدة افعال لا يجب فعلها.

السادس عشر. لاجل نصراني له سرية ويتزوج عليها.

السابع عشر. لاجل الامرأة الحرة وما تفعله.

الثامن عشر. لاجل القوابل وانعزال الرجال عن النساء في الصلاة والعذارى يغطين رؤوسهن ولاجل النساء اللاتي يلدن.

التاسع عشر. لاجل متعظ يقتل على الاستشهاد قبل المعمودية يدفن مع الشهداء ولاجل المتعظين والشروط التي يعملها المتعظون عند المعمودية والاستحلاف وترتيب قداس المعمودية وتقديس قداس الجسد والدم.

العشرون. لاجل صوم الاربعاء والجمعة والاربعين.

الحادي والعشرون. لاجل اجتماع جميع الكهنة والشعب الى الكنيسة كل يوم.

الثاني والعشرون. لاجل الاسبوع الذي للفصح الذي لليهود يتجنب فيه الفرح ولاجل ما يؤكل فيه ولاجل من كان في غربة ولم يعرف البصخة.

الثالث والعشرون. لاجل التعليم انه اعظم من البحر ويجب السعي في طلبه.

الرابع والعشرون. لاجل افتقاد الاسقف للمرضى واذا صلى مريض في كنيسة وله بيت يمضي اليه.

The fourteenth: a Christian is not to become a soldier.

The fifteenth: a number of acts which should not be performed.

The sixteenth: concerning a Christian who has a concubine and marries other than her.

The seventeenth: concerning a free woman and what she should do.

The eighteenth: concerning midwives and the segregation of men from women at prayer, that virgins should cover their heads; and concerning women who have given birth.

The nineteenth: concerning a catechumen who is killed on account of witnessing before baptism, that he is to be buried with the martyrs; concerning catechumens and the qualifications that they fulfil during baptism and the exorcism and the ordering of the liturgy of baptism and the consecratory liturgy of the Body and the Blood.

The twentieth: concerning the fast of Wednesday, and Friday, and Lent.[5]

The twenty-first: concerning the gathering of the assembled priesthood and the people at the church each day.

The twenty-second: concerning the week of the Passover of the Jews, during which rejoicing is to be avoided; and concerning what is eaten then; and concerning somebody who was abroad and did not know about the Pascha (πάσχα).[6]

The twenty-third: concerning instruction, that it is greater than the sea and that one should be eager in its pursuit.[7]

The twenty-fourth: concerning the visit of the bishop to the sick; when a sick person has prayed in church, and has a home, he should go there.

---

5   Literally, "the forty."
6   See the note in the chapter heading ad loc.
7   Reading ṭālabhu. R here reads ṭāʾthu, "submission" or "docility", a not impossible reading, though ṭālabhu is found in the chapter heading.

الخامس والعشرون. لاجل اقامة وكيل المرضى من قبل الاسقف ولاجل اوقات الصلاة.

السادس والعشرون. لاجل استماع الكلام في الكنيسة والصلاة فيها.

السابع والعشرون. لاجل من لا يمضي الى الكنيسة كل يوم يقرأ الكتب. واي وقت صليت فأغسل يديك. والحث على الصلاة نصف الليل وفي وقت صياح الديك.

الثامن والعشرون. لا يذق أحد من المؤمنين شيئا الا بعد ان تناول السرائر لا سيما في ايام الصوم.

التاسع والعشرون. لاجل حراسة المذبح لئلا يقع شيء في الكأس وان لا يسقط شيء من الكهنة والمؤمنين لئلا يتسلط عليه روح خبيث ولا يتكلم أحد في الستارة الا صلاة واذا فرغوا مما يدفعوا للشعب يكن كلمن يدخل الى الموضع يقرأ المزامير عوضا من الجلاجل ولاجل رشم الصليب وتراب المذبح يلقى في التيار.

الثلاثون. لاجل المتعظين.

الحادي والثلاثون. لاجل الاسقف والقسيس اذا آمرا الشماس ان يقرب الشعب فيقرب.

الثاني والثلاثون. لاجل العذارى والارامل يصمن ويصلين في الكنيسة. الاكليركسات يصوموا باختيارهم والاسقف لا يربط بصوم الا مع الاكليرس. ولاجل وليمة او عشاء يصلح للفقراء.

الثالث والثلاثون. لاجل انالمسيس يصنعونه الذين ماتوا ولا يكن ذلك في يوم الأحد.

The twenty-fifth: concerning the institution[8] of a steward for the sick by the bishop and concerning the times of prayer.

The twenty-sixth: concerning the hearing of the word in the church, and the prayers therein.

The twenty-seventh: concerning anyone who does not[9] go to church each day, that he should read the Scripture. Whenever you pray, so wash your hands. And the exhortation to prayer in the middle of the night, and at the time of cock-crow.

The twenty-eighth: that none of the faithful should taste of anything until after he has received the mysteries, especially not on the days of fasting.

The twenty-ninth: concerning vigilance at the altar,[10] that nothing should fall in the cup, and that nothing should fall on account of the priests or on account of the faithful, lest a wicked spirit should have power over it. And nobody should speak within the veil except for prayer. And when they finish communicating the congregation. When they enter the (holy) place they read psalms instead of the bells. And concerning marking with the cross. And the dust of the altar is to be thrown into the stream.

The thirtieth: concerning the catechumens.

The thirty-first: concerning the bishop and the presbyter, when they instruct the deacon to communicate the people, and he communicates.

The thirty-second: concerning the virgins and the widows, fasting and praying in the church; that the clergy (κληρικός) fast at their discretion, and the bishop is not bound to fast except with the clergy (κλῆρος); concerning a dinner or a feast suitable for the poor.

The thirty-third: concerning the ἀνάλημψις which is kept for those who have died, and that this should not be on the first day.

---

8   This word is lacking in R.
9   All witnesses omit this negative, which is incorporated following the canon.
10  K reads: "vigilance over the offerings which are on the altar."

الرابع والثلاثون. لاجل انه لا يتكلم احد كثيرا ولا يصيح ولاجل دخول القديسين الى منازل المؤمنين.

الخامس والثلاثون. لاجل شماس حاضر في وليمة وليس قسيس حاضرا يكن عوضا منه في الصلاة وكسر الخبز للبركة وليس للجسد واصراف الارامل قبل العشاء.

السادس والثلاثون. لاجل ابكار اثمار الارض واول اندرهم ومعاصرهم والزيت والعسل واللبن والصوف وغير ذلك مما يمضي به الى الاسقف ليبارك عليه.

السابع والثلاثون. لاجل كل دفعة ينال الاسقف السرائر تجتمع الشمامسة والقساء وهم لابسون ثيابا بيضا ابهى من كل الشعب وكذلك الاغنستسيون.

الثامن والثلاثون. لاجل الليلة التي قام فيها سيدنا لا ينم احد في تلك الليلة ويستحم بالماء ولاجل من يخطأ بعد المعمودية وشرح ذلك والنهي عما لا يجب وفعل ما يجب واذا اراد الانسان يتشبه بالملائكة.

Ναι πε πεκανων ντεκκλησια νταϥϭϩαϊϲου νχϭι ιππολιτος παρχεπισκοπος ετουααβ ν̄ϩρωμη

هذه هي قوانين الكنيسة الوصايا التي كتبها ابوليدس مقدم اساقفة رومية كأوامر الرسل من جهة سيدنا المسيح الناطق فيه

The thirty-fourth: concerning the matter that nobody should talk overmuch or call out; and concerning the entry of the saints into the homes of the faithful.

The thirty-fifth: concerning a deacon present at a supper, and no presbyter is present, he is to take his place for the prayer and for the breaking of bread and the blessing, but not for the body; and the dismissal of widows before the evening.

The thirty-sixth: concerning the first-fruits of the earth, and the first of their threshing-floors and presses, and the oil, the milk, the honey, the wool, and the other things that should be taken to the bishop for his blessing on them.

The thirty-seventh: concerning each occasion on which the bishop offers[11] the mysteries, the deacons and the presbyters are to meet dressed in white garments more glorious than the people; and also the readers (ἀναγνώστης).

The thirty-eighth: concerning the night on which Our Lord rose; that nobody should sleep on that night, and they should bathe in water; concerning anyone who sins after baptism, and the explanation of that, and the prohibition of what should not be done, and the performance of what should be done; and if a person desires to be an imitator of the angels.

Coptic:[12] These are the canons (κανών) of the church (ἐκκλησία) which Hippolytus, archbishop (ἀρχιεπίσκοπος) of Rome, wrote.

Arabic: These are the canons (κανών) of the church, the precepts which Hippolytus, archbishop of Rome, wrote in accordance with the traditions of the apostles, through Our Lord the Christ,[13] speaking in him.

---

11   Literally "takes"; a mistranslation of Coptic ϫⲓ.
12   This Coptic title is actually found not in any MS of the *Canones* but is supplied by Coquin from a manuscript of the *Sententiae* of Nicaea!
13   m has "the Holy Spirit."

## القانون الاول
### لاجل الامانة المقدسة

قبل كل شيء نتكلم لاجل الامانة المقدسة الصحيحة بسيدنا يسوع المسيح ابن الله الحي. ووضعناه بامانة ونحن راضيون بكل ثبات ونقول نحن ان الثالوث المساوية التامة في الكرامة متساوية في المجد وليس له ابتداء ولا انتهاء الكلمة ابن الله وهو خالق كل البريه ما يرى وما لا يرى. هذا وضعناه ونحن راضيون بحق بهم.

والذين جسروا وتكلموا بما لا يجب لاجل كلمة الله كما تكلم لاجل هؤلاء سيدنا يسوع المسيح فاجتمعنا بالاكثر جدا بقوة الله وافرقناهم لانهم ما هم متفقون مع الكتب المقدسة نطق الله ولا معنا نحن تلاميذ الكتب. فلاجل هذا افرقناهم من الكنيسة وجعلنا امرهم لله الذي يدين كل البرية بالعدل.

والذين هم غير عارفين هؤلاء نعلمهم إياه بلا حسد لئلا يسقطوا في موت سوء كهراطيق بل يستحقوا الحياة الابدية ويكونوا يعلموا اولادهم ومن يأتي بعدهم هذه الامانة المقدسة.

## The first canon:
## concerning the sanctified faith

Before all else we speak of the sacred and authentic faith in our Lord Jesus Christ, the Son of the living God, and this we have established in fidelity, and we hold it in all certainty, and we state that the Trinity is equal and perfect in honour, is equal in glory, and there is no beginning or end to the Word, and he created all that is, visible and invisible.[14] This we have established and to this we truly hold.

As to those who have dared speak what is not fitting concerning the word of God: as our Lord Jesus Christ spoke concerning them we assembled in the great power of God, we removed them because they were not in accordance with the Scripture, the word of God, nor with us, the disciples of the Scripture. On this account we removed them from the church and committed them to God, who judges every creature uprightly.

We teach this things to those who are ignorant of them, without malice, so that they do not plunge themselves into a terrible death, like the heretics (αἱρετικός), but should prove worthy of eternal life, and teach this, the holy faith,[15] to their children and to those who succeed them.

---

14 Col 1:16. However, the phrase enters a number of fourth-century creeds, attributing the creation to the Father (Nicaea, 325), or to the Father through the Son (first creed of Antioch, 341; fourth creed of Antioch, 341; the Makrostichos creed, 345; Constantinople, 360).
15 m reads "single faith."

## القانون الثاني
### لاجل الاساقفة

الاسقف يختار من جميع الشعب ويكون بلا وجد كما هو مكتوب لاجله في الرسول. وفي الاسبوع الذي يقسم فيه يقول كل الاكليرس والشعب انا نؤثره ويكون سكوت في كل الماشية من بعد الاكساملوجيدس ويصلوا الكل عليه وقولوا يا الله هذا الذي اعددته لنا.

ويختاروا واحدا من الاساقفة والقساء ويجعل يده على رأسه ويصلي ويقول.

## القانون الثالث
### الصلاة على من يصير اسقفا وترتيب القداس

يا الله أبا سيدنا يسوع المسيح أبا الرحمات وإله كل عزاء الساكن في العلاء وينظر المتواضعين العالم بكل شيء قبل ان يكون انت الذي حددت حدود الكنيسة الذي آمر من أدم ان يدوم جنس عدل من جهة الاسقف هذا الذي هو الكبير ابرهيم الذي يقيم الرئاسات والسلاطين انظر الى فلان بقوتك وروح قادرة هذا الذي دفعته الرسل المقدسين من جهة ربنا يسوع المسيح ابنك الوحيد. هؤلاء الذين اسسوا الكنيسة في كل موضع كرامة ومجدا لاسمك القدوس.

## The second canon: concerning the bishop

The bishop is elected by the entire gathering of the people,[16] and is to be without blame, as is said of him in the apostle.[17] And on the sabbath when he is installed,[18] all the clergy (κλῆρος) and people[19] say: "We choose him." There is silence in the flock after the confession (ἐξομολόγησις),[20] and all pray for him and say: "O God, this is the one you have chosen for us." And they shall choose one of the bishops and presbyters and he shall lay his hand upon his head and pray, and say:

## The third canon: the prayer upon the one who becomes bishop and the ordering of the liturgy

O God, Father of Our Lord Jesus Christ, Father of mercies, and God of all solace, dwelling on high and looking on the lowly, knowing all things before they come to be, who fixed boundaries for the church, who from Adam[21] decreed that there should be a righteous race, through the means of this bishop, that is [the race] of the great Abraham, who have established authorities and powers, look upon N[22] with your strength, and the Spirit of governance[23] which you bestowed on the holy apostles through our Lord Jesus Christ, your only Son. They are those who founded the church in every place, the honour and glory of your holy name.

---

16 The phrase might also mean *from* all the people. The same phenomenon is observable in the Sahidic version of *Traditio apostolica*.
17 1 Tim 3:2; Titus 1:6-7.
18 The phrase more naturally means "during the week." However it is almost certainly a rendition of ϩⲙ̄ ⲡⲥⲁⲃⲃⲁⲧⲟⲛ. The use of Saturday evening as a liturgical occasion is well attested in Egypt (thus note Socrates *Hist. Eccl.* 5.22) and in Asia (*Vit. Pol.* 22), this latter reference being particularly significant since this is the occasion of an episcopal election and ordination.
19 m has simply "people."
20 As Coquin notes, this is hardly the right word. He attributes the confusion to the Coptic translator, suggesting ἀνθομολόγησις as a possible intended word. Achelis, *Ältesten Quellen*, 184-185, takes this to mean a confession of sins prior to worship (such as in *Did.* 14.1), but the context will not allow this.
21 Adam (*ā'dam*) is an error almost certainly caused through mishearing *qidam* (beginning), the reading one would expect on the basis of *Traditio apostolica*.
22 m adds "your servant".
23 Ps 51:12 (50:14) (an allusion also found in the Hippolytean original).

لانك عارف بقلب كل احد اجعل له أن يرعى شعبك بلا خطيئة ليستحق ان يرعى رعيتك العظيمة المقدسة وتجعل سيرته اعلى من كل شعبه بلا اعتراض وتجعله محسودا بالصلاح من كل أحد وتقبل صلواته وقرابينه التي يرفعها لك نهارا وليلا وتكن لك رائحة ذكية. وتعطيه يا رب الاسقفية وروحا رحيمة وسلطانا لغفران الذنوب وتعطيه قوة ان يحل كل رباط ظلم الشياطين ويشفي الاعلا وترضض ابليس تحت قدميه سريعا. بسيدنا يسوع المسيح هذا الذي من جهته المجد لك معه والروح القدس الى أبد الابدين. آمين.

ويقول كل الشعب آمين.

وبعد هذا يلتفتوا اليه كلهم ويقبلوه بسلام لانه يستحقه.

والشماس يأتي بالقرابين ويضع الذي يده على القرابين مع القساء ويقول.

او كيريوس ماطا بنطن.

فيقول الشعب ومع روحك.

ويقول أنا ايمون دسقردياس.

فيقول اخومن ابرستنكيريون.

فيقول اوخارستيسومن طو كيريوس.

فيقال اكسيون كا ديكآون الذي هو مستحق.

وبعد ذلك يقول الصلاة ويكمل القداس.

Since you know the heart of all,[24] grant that he may watch over your people, without stain, may he deserve to watch over your great and sanctified flock, make his life indisputably[25] better than that of all the people, make him envied by all on account of his goodness. And receive his prayers and offerings which he lifts up to you day and night; may they be a sweet scent to you.[26] And grant, Lord, the episcopate: a merciful spirit and the power to forgive sins, and grant him the authority to release every bond of demonic oppression, to heal the sick, and to trample the devil swiftly under his feet.[27] Through Our Lord Jesus Christ, through whom the glory is yours, with him and the Holy Spirit, to the ages of the ages. Amen.

And all the people say "Amen."

And after this they all turn to him and kiss him in peace since he is worthy.

And the deacon brings the offering, and the one who has become bishop puts his hands on the offerings, with the presbyters, and says:

"The Lord be with all." (ὁ Κύριος μετὰ πάντων)[28]

So the people say "And with your spirit."

He says "Lift up your hearts." (ἄνω ὑμῶν τὰς καρδίας)

So they say: "We have them with the Lord." (ἔχομεν πρὸς τὸν Κύριον)

So he says "Let us give thanks to the Lord." (εὐχαριστήσωμεν[29] τῷ Κυρίῳ)

So they say "It is fitting and just." (ἄξιον καὶ δίκαιον) That is to say, "it is fitting."

After this he says the prayer and completes the liturgy.

---

24 Acts 1:24 (an allusion also found in the Hippolytean original).
25 Following a suggestion of Rifaat Ebied, reading *i'tirāḍ* with d rather than *i'rāḍ* (read by Coquin following the other witnesses). This would mean "without reluctance".
26 Gen 8:21.
27 Rom 16:20. Bradshaw notes the appearance of this phrase in the Coptic Orthodox liturgy in prayers for the patriarch (to be found at Brightman, *Liturgies eastern and western*, 161, 171. He suggests a common euchological tradition.
28 The same greeting is found in the (Egyptian) *Liturgy of St Mark*.
29 R has εὐχαριστῶμεν.

وان كان زيت يصلي عليه هكذا وان كان ليس هم هذه الفصول الواحدة بل هي قوة واحدة. وان كانوا ابكار شيء من الماكول أتى بهم واحد واحد فيصلي عليه ويبارك على الثمرة التي بيؤتى له منها في صلاته.

وفي كل صلاة تقال على كل شيء فيقال في آخر الصلاة المجد لك ايها الاب والابن والروح القدس الى ابد الابدين. آمين.

### القانون الرابع
### لاجل قسمة القساء

واذا اقسم قسيس فليفعل به مثل كلما يفعل بالاسقف ما خلا الجلوس على الكرسي. ويصلوا عليه صلاة الاسقف كلها ما خلا اسم الاسقف وحده.

ويكون الاسقف يعادل القسيس في كل شيء ما خلا اسم الكرسي والقسمة لانه لم يدفع له سلطان ان يقسم.

### القانون الخامس
### لاجل قسمة الشمامسة

واذا اقسم شماس فيفعل به كالقوانين الواجدة ويقواوا هذه الصلاة عليه.

وليس انه يقام للقسيسية بل للشماسية كخادم لله. ويخدم الاسقف والقساء في كل شيء وليس في شيء في وقت القداس وحده بل ويخدم المرضى من الشعب هؤلاء الذين ليس لهم ناس ويعرف الاسقف ليصلي عليهم او يدفع لهم ما يحتاجون اليه او لقوم مستورين ايضا محتاجين.

And if there is oil he prays over it likewise, even if not with the same expression, but with the same meaning. If there are first-fruits, anything that is edible, that somebody has brought, he prays for him,[30] and in his prayer he blesses the fruit which has been brought to him.

And in every prayer said on each item, at the end of the prayer is said: Glory to you, Father, and the Son, and the Holy Spirit, to the ages of the ages. Amen.

## The fourth canon:
### concerning the ordination of presbyters

When a presbyter is ordained it is done for him entirely the same as it is done for a bishop, apart from the seating on the throne. And they pray over him the entire (ordination) prayer of a bishop, solely apart from the name of the bishop.

The bishop is equal in all things to the presbyter,[31] except the throne, and (the power of) ordination, since the authority of ordination is not given to him.

## The fifth canon:
### concerning the ordination of deacons

When a deacon is ordained it is performed in accordance with the same[32] canons (κανών) and they say this prayer over him.

He is not ordained to the presbyterate but to the diaconate, as one who serves God. And he shall serve the bishop and the presbyters in all things, not only on the occasion of the liturgy but shall serve those of the congregation who are sick, those who have nobody, and make this known to the bishop so that he may pray for them, or supply them with what they need, or also those who are concealed yet may be in need.

---

30  "For him" or "over him" or "over it" (the fruit.) There is no way of telling which was originally intended.
31  Coquin suggests that the terms should be reversed: "The presbyter is equal in all things to the bishop."
32  Literally "the only canons", a misreading of Coptic ⲟⲩⲱⲧ which, depending on context, could have either meaning.

ويخدموا الاخر الذين لهم رحمة الاساقفة ويمكنهم ان يدفعوا للارامل واليتامى والفقراء. ويكمل كل الخدم هكذا. هذا حقا هو الشماس الذي المسيح قال لاجله ان الذي يخدمني آبي يكرمه.

ويضع الاسقف يده عليه ويقول هذه الصلاة عليه قائلا:

يا الله آبا سيدنا يسوع المسيح نبتهل اليك ان تفيض روحك القدس على فلان وتعده مع الذين يخدمونك كارادتك كلها مثل استفانس والذين معه. وتملاه قوة وحكمة مثل استفانس وتجعل له ان يظفر بكل قوات المحال بمثال صليبك الذي ترشمه فيه وتجعل سيرته ان يكون بلا خطيئة امام كل الناس وتعليما لكثير ليخلص خلقا في الكنيسة المقدسة بلا عثرة وتقبل كل خدمته. بربنا يسوع المسيح هذا الذي من جهته المجد لك معه والروح القدس الى ابد الابدين. آمين.

They[33] are also to serve those who receive episcopal charity, being able to supply the widows, the orphans, the destitute. All this is his service. Thus it is indeed the deacon of whom Christ said "Whoever serves me will be honoured by the Father."[34]

And the bishop places his hand upon him and says this prayer over him, saying:

O God, Father of Our Lord Jesus Christ, we ask you to pour out your Holy Spirit on N and so count him with those who serve you entirely in accordance with your will, like Stephen and those who were with him. Fill him with power and wisdom, like Stephen,[35] and grant that he may triumph over the powers of the evil one through the sign of your cross with which you mark him, making his life sinless in the sight of all people, and a lesson for many, that he may save a multitude faultlessly within the holy church, and receive all his service through our master Jesus Christ, through whom be glory to you, with him and the Holy Spirit, to the ages of the ages. Amen.

---

33   Coquin suggests that this sudden plural reflects a Coptic passive. His reconstruction of a possible text is: "what forms the episcopal charity be distributed, and that it be supplied to the widows..."
34   John 12:26.
35   Acts 6:8.

### القانون السادس
### لاجل الذين يعاقبون على الامانة المقدسة

اذا استحق واحد ان يقف في محفل لاجل الامانة ويحتمل العقوبة لاجل المسيح وبعد هذا يتخلص بنعمة المراحم هذا هكذا استحق رتبة القسيسية من جهة الله لا يقسم من جهة الاسقف فان اعترافه هو قسمته. فاذا صير اسقفا فليقسم.

واذا كان واحد اعترف ولم يؤلم بعقوبة فقد استحق القسيسية ولكن يقسم من جهة الاسقف.

واذا كان هو عبد واحد احتمل عقوبة لاجل المسيح هذا هكذا هو قسيس الماشية. وان كان لم ينل شكل القسيسية بل نال روح القسيسية.

والاسقف ليس يصلي بتلاوة بل من جهة الروح القدس.

## The sixth canon:
## concerning those who are punished for the holy faith

If anyone should be worthy of appearing before a court on account of faith, and endures punishment on account of Christ, and is thereafter, by gracious mercy, set free, he is thus worthy of the order[36] of presbyterate from God, and is not ordained by the bishop, his confession being his ordination. If he subsequently becomes a bishop, then he is ordained.

If there is somebody who confesses, but does not suffer any penalty, he is certainly deserving of the presbyterate, but he should be ordained by the bishop.

If there is somebody who is a slave, who endures a penalty on account of Christ, he is by this means a presbyter of the flock. Even if he does not receive the form[37] of presbyterate, he nonetheless receives the spirit of presbyterate.

The bishop should not pray through recitation, but by the Holy Spirit.[38]

---

36  The Arabic *rutba* might represent τάξις or κλῆρος.
37  Arabic *šakl*, meaning outward appearance, form, or shape. Coquin suggests that the Greek might originally have been σφραγίς, though τύπος is also a possibility.
38  Riedel is puzzled by this statement, thinking that it refers back to the bishop's power of ordination. However, parallel witnesses in versions of *Traditio apostolica* clarify its meaning.

## القانون السابع

### لاجل اصطفاء الاغنستس والابودياقن

اذا اصطفى اغنستس تكون له فضائل الشماس. ولا تجعل اليد عليه اولا بل يدفع له الاسقف الانجيل.

والابودياقن على هذا الترتيب ولا يقسم وهو بتول وان كان ليس له زوجة الا ان يشهد له ويزكي مع جهة جيران له انه بعيد من النساء في زمان قامته.

ولا توضع يد على انسان كبتول الا ان يبلغ قامته ويدخل الى كبر ويثمن اذا شهد له.

الابودياقن والاغنستس اذا صليا وحدهما يقفا خلف ويكون الابودياقن يخدم خلف الشماس.

The seventh canon:
concerning the selection of the reader (ἀναγνώστης)
and the subdeacon (ὑποδιάκων)

If a reader (ἀναγνώστης) is selected, his conduct should be like that of a deacon. A hand is not laid on him, but first the bishop gives him the Gospel.

And the subdeacon (ὑποδιάκων) after this order. He is not to be ordained whilst celibate and if he has no wife unless someone bears witness to him, and is supported by his neighbours, that he has kept aloof from women[39] during the time of his adulthood.

A hand should not be laid on anyone as a celibate who has not attained adulthood, or is reaching maturity;[40] he is given consideration when witness is borne on his behalf.[41]

The subdeacon (ὑποδιάκων) and the reader (ἀναγνώστης), when they pray by themselves,[42] are stationed to the rear, and the subdeacon (ὑποδιάκων) serves to the rear of the deacon.[43]

---

39   m reads "venality."
40   Coquin notes that there is considerable variety among the manuscripts in the diacritical points given to this word, leading to uncertainty regarding its meaning.
41   Achelis suggests that this paragraph, and that part of the previous paragraph relating to the celibacy of a subdeacon has been misplaced, and belongs with the provisions regarding widows. There is something in this, as *Traditio apostolica* has a provision regarding virgins which is not found in *Canones Hippolyti*. It is indeed possible that something has dropped out in the transmission, though one suspects that the omission occurred in *Traditio apostolica* prior to its redaction into *Canones Hippolyti*, and that the redactor has thus sought to make sense of a puzzling provision by applying it to the subdeacon.
42   Although this provision seems to apply to liturgical arrangements, it is possible that the statement regarding these officials praying "by themselves" originally intended that their sole ministry was prayer, an adaptation of the statement in *Trad. ap.* 10.5 that the widow is not ordained as she is appointed for prayer alone, one of a series of provisions (including the statement at *Trad. ap.* 13 that the subdeacon follows the deacon) denying ordination by handlaying to a number of roles. μόνον, an adverb in the Greek might be rendered into Coptic as ⲙⲟⲛⲟⲛ, and then taken as referring to the deacon and subdeacon (the Coptic being indeclinable.) One also wonders whether *idha*, "when" or "if", here represents ⲉⲣϣⲁⲛ-, intended to mean "since" and taken in its conditional sense by the Arabic translator.
43   So R. d reads "in front of the deacon", m "in front of the people."

القانون الثامن

لاجل مواهب الشفاء

اذا سأل واحد عن قسمه ويقول اني نلت موهبة الشفاء لا يقسم إلا بعد ان يظهر الامر وهل الشفاء الذي يكون من جهته هو من قبل الله.

وقسيس اذا ولدت زوجته لا يقطع.

## The eighth canon:
## concerning gifts of healing

If anyone should request ordination, and say "I have received a gift of healing" he should not be ordained until after the matter is obvious, and that the healing which has come about through him is of God.[44]

And a presbyter should not be excluded when his wife has given birth.

---

[44] Bradshaw, *Canons*, 16, reads this rewriting of a provision from *Traditio apostolica* as indicating that healing is to be a preserve of the ordained. Barrett-Lennard, "Canons of Hippolytus", 148, by contrast, suggests that this indicates that a cadre of lay healers was recognized by the bishop. My own reading is simply that healing as a charism might be seen as the basis for ordination, but that this does not mean that there is an organized "cadre" of healers, rather that charismatic healing, alongside other gifts, is known in this community. The issue is solved elsewhere through the establishment of an order of exorcists (*Const. ap.* 8.26.1-3.)

القانون التاسع

لاجل قسيس يسكن في موضع ليس له ولاجل كرامة الارامل

قسيس اذا مضى وسكن في مواضع ليست له ويقبله اكليرس ذلك الموضع فليسألوا اسقف كرسيه لئلا يكون هرب لاجل سبب. فان كانت مدينته بعيدة فليجرب ان كان هو تلميذا اولا هذا هو مثال القساء وبعد ذلك يشارك ويعطى كرامة مضاعفة.

ولا تقسم بعد الارامل اللاتي يقمن فان كانت لهن الوصايا التي للرسول فلا يقسمن بل يصلي عليهن لان القسمة هي للذكور. وكرامة الارامل اكثر من كل ما يكون لهن من كثرة الصلاة وخدمة المرضى وصوم كثير.

The ninth canon:
concerning a presbyter who dwells in a place not his own, and
concerning the honour due to widows[45]

If a presbyter departs to live in a place which is not his own and the clergy (κλῆρος) of that place receive him they should ask the bishop of his see in case he is fleeing for some reason.[46]

If his town is distant they should examine whether he is learned,[47] for this is the mark of a presbyter, and thereafter he may participate and receive a double honour.[48]

Nor yet should the widows who are established be ordained, for there are commands of the apostle regarding them,[49] that they are not to ordain but to pray for them, since ordination is for men. The honour of widows is very great, because of all that they have to do: frequent prayer, ministry to the sick, and much fasting.[50]

---

45  The title is translated very literally. The phrase "in a place not his own" is a Copticism for "a strange (ἀλλοτρίος) place". The "honour due to widows" is rendered by Coquin as "la fonction des veuves", though the underlying Greek for the word rendered "fonction" is certainly τιμή, an allusion to 1 Tim 5:3.
46  Cf. the sixteenth canon of Nicaea, which expressly forbids any presbyter or deacon from moving from one church to another.
47  Literally "a disciple". A confusion between μαθητευθείς and μαθητής has entered the chain of transmission.
48  1 Tim 5:17.
49  Coquin and Bradshaw each cite 1 Tim 5:3-15. Although this concerns widows, it does not describe their duties as given here, which, as Bradshaw (16) notes, are more akin to those of *Apostolic church order* and the *Didascalia*; in agreeing with this we may also note that *Testamentum Domini* provides significant parallels for the activity of widows in this regard. Ultimately this is an adaptation of *Trad. ap.* 10.4-5, in which it is stated that ordination is on account of a liturgy, and thus that widows are not ordained because their task is prayer, rather than liturgy. Thus the citation of the "apostle" may be as much to 1 Cor 14:34.
50  Cf. *Apostolic church order* 21: "Three widows should be appointed. Two are to continue in prayer for all who are in temptation and for revelations concerning whatever is necessary. One is to assist women who are being troubled by sickness."

### القانون العاشر
### لاجل الذين يصيرون نصارى

الذين يسعون الى الكنيسة ليصيروا نصارى ليجربوا بكل ثبات ولاجل اي سبب رفضوا بخدمتهم لئلا يدخلوا هزؤا. فان كان أتي بامانة صحيحة فليقبل بفرح ويسأل عن صنعته ويعلم من جهة الشماس. هكذا يكون معلما في الكتب ليجحد ابليس وخدمته كلها وكل الزمان الذي يوعط فيه من قبل يعد مع الشعب.

فان كان هو عبدا ومولاه وثنيا ويمنعه مولاه فلا يعمد بل يرضى انه نصراني. وان مات ولم ينل الموهبة فانه لا يفرق من الماشية.

## The tenth canon:
### concerning those who become Christians

Those who enter the church to become Christians should be very rigorously examined as to their reasons for abandoning their practice,[51] so that they may not enter as a joke. If he comes in good faith he should be received with joy and should be examined regarding his profession, and should be instructed by the deacon. Thus he shall be instructed in the Scriptures, that he should renounce the Devil and all his service; and all the time that he is being instructed, he is from then on counted among the people.

If he is a slave, and his master is a pagan, and his master forbids him, he is not to be baptized; it is sufficient that he is a Christian. If he dies, and has not received the gift, he is yet not separated from the flock.

---

51 Literally "their service." Coquin suggests that this is an attempt to render ϣⲙ̄ϣⲉ (λατρεία); the translation attempts to capture this.

### القانون الحادي عشر

**لاجل من يعمل الاصنام والاوثان صانعا كان او مصورا**

كل صائغ فليعلم ان لا يعمل وثنا أصلا ولا شيئا من الاصنام صانعا كان او عاملا للفضة او مصورا او بقية الصنائع. اذا وجدوا من بعد المعمودية انهم يصنعون شيئا هكذا ما خلا ما يحتاجون الناس اليه ليفرقوا الى ان يتوبوا.

## The eleventh canon:
### concerning those who make images and idols, whether they be craftsmen or painters

Every jeweller[52] should be so instructed that he should not make any idol, nor any image, whether he be a craftsman, a silversmith, or a painter, or any other manufacturer. If, after baptism, they are found to be making anything of this nature, apart from what people need, they are to be excluded until they do penance.[53]

---

52  The word for jeweller, ṣā'iġ, (which also renders "goldsmith") and that for craftsman, ṣāni', are easily confused in Arabic. At various points within this canon and its title the witnesses betray such confusion. Although Coquin is followed here, it is quite likely that this word should read "craftsman", and "craftsman" in the next line should be "jeweller" or "goldsmith."

53  d reads "desist."

### القانون الثاني عشر
### النهي عن عدة افعال لا يقبل فاعلها الا بعد التوبة

كل من يصير تادرس او مصارعا او من يجري او يعلم ملاهي او من يهزأ قدام البومسيا او معلم التوحش او كنيكس او بولوطس او محارب مع الوحوش او كاهن الاصنام هؤلاء كلهم لا يبعثوا لهم كلاما مقدسا الا ان يتطهروا أولا من هذه الافعال الطمثة. ومن بعد اربعين يوما يستمعوا الكلام فان كانوا مستحقين فيتعمدوا. ومعلم الكنيسة هو الذي يجرب هذا لفعل.

اغرماديكوس يعلم الصبيان الصغار إن كان ليس له معاش يعيش به الا هذا فليؤدب اذا أظهر في كل وقت للذين يعلمهم ويعترف أنهم شياطين هؤلاء الذين سموهم الامم انهم الهة ويقول امامهم كل يوم ان ليس اله الا الاب والابن والروح القدس. وان كان يمكنه ان يعلم تلاميذه كلام كثير الابواادس وان كان يمكنه بالاكثر ان يعلمهم امانة كلام الحق بهذا تكون له أجر.

## The twelfth canon:
## the prohibition of several acts, and that whoever does them will not be accepted without repentance

Anyone who happens to be a theatrical agent (θεατρώνης), or a wrestler, or a runner, or teaches music, or jives before the processions (πομπεία),[54] or teaches gladiatorial arts,[55] or a hunter (κυνηγός), or a hairdresser (πωλεύτης), or someone who fights with wild beasts, or a priest of idols, to none of these is the holy word to be revealed until first they have been purified from these filthy acts. Thereafter they shall hear the word for forty days,[56] and be baptized if they are worthy. It is the teacher of the church who tests this matter.

A schoolteacher (γραμματικός) who teaches small children, if he has no livelihood by which to earn apart from that, should instruct, as long as he makes it clear at all times to those he is teaching and directs that those whom the nations call gods are demons,[57] and states before them each day that there is no God apart from the Father, the Son, and the Holy Spirit. And if he can teach his pupils the many words of the poets (ποιητής), and better still can teach them the faith of the word of truth, then he will be rewarded for this.

---

54  Coquin's conjecture; the Arabic is far from clear due to confusion over diacritical points.
55  Again Coquin's suggestion; the Arabic literally states "teaches the art of savagery."
56  Coquin suggests that this should not be taken as Lent, as there is no evidence that paschal baptism is normal in this community. See further n. 83 below on the subject of paschal baptism.
57  An allusion to Ps 96:5 (95:5).

القانون الثالث عشر

لاجل سلطان او جندي لا يقتلوا احدا ولو اومروا ولا يلبسوا تيجانا ومن له رئاسة ولا يفعل العدل الذي في الانجيل يفرق ولا يصلي مع الاسقف

انسان نال سلطان القتل او جندي فلا يقتلوا جملة ولو أومروا ان يقتلوا. ولا يلفظوا بكلمة سوء. ولا يلبسوا تيجانا على رؤوسهم الذين نالوا علامة.

كل انسان ينال رفعة رئاسة مقدم او سلطانة ولم يلبس العدل الذي للانجيل فليفرق من الماشية ولا يصلي معه الاسقف.

The thirteenth canon:
concerning a magistrate or a soldier, that they are not to kill anyone, even if they are ordered; and they are not to wear crowns; and anyone who has authority, and does not perform the uprightness which is of the Gospel should be separated and is not to pray with the bishop

Anyone who has received the power to put to death, or a soldier, should not kill at all, even if they are ordered to kill. They are not to utter a bad word.[58] They are not to wear crowns on their heads when they receive an honour.

Anyone who is raised to the authority of a prefect or a magistrate, and is not vested[59] with the uprightness of the Gospel, should be excluded from the flock, and the bishop should not pray with him.

---

58   Coquin suggests that this is a prohibition of oaths. The context suggests, however, that it may provide a warning to a magistrate not to pronounce a capital sentence.
59   Literally "did not wear"; Coquin suggests a confusion deriving from the similarity between the negated perfect and the negated durative present in Coptic.

### القانون الرابع عشر
### لا يصير نصراني جنديا

لايمض نصراني يصير جنديا الا أن يلزمه قائد له السيف. ولا يدع عليه وزر دم. فاذا اهرق دما فلا يتناول من السرائر الا أن يتطهر بأدب وبكاء ونحيب. ولا تكن تقدمته بخداع بل بخوف الله.

### القانون الخامس عشر
### عده الفعال لا يجب فعلها

زان او من يأكل من حق الزناء او مؤنث ولا سيما من يتكلم بدغل او واحد عاجز او اسطوس او ساحر او منجم او عراف او مفسر الاحلام او حاو او مفتن يفتن الجماعة او من يعمل الفاقطيريات او مراب او ظالم او محب للعالم او محب للايمان اي الاقسام او من ينكر الناس او من يرائي او مزدري بالناس او من يختار الساعات والايام انها مذمومة هولاء كلهم وما يشبههم لا تعظوهم ولا تعمدهم الا بعد ان يكفوا عن هذه الافعال كلها هكذا ويشهد لهم من ثلثة شهود انهم قد انكفوا عن هذه الرذائل كلها لانه ربما كان الانسان يبقى في اغراضه الى شيخوخته الا ان يقوى بقوة عظيمة.

واذا وجدوا من بعد المعمودية في هذه الرذائل التي هي هكذا فليخرجوا من الكنيسة حتى يتوبوا ببكاء وصوم ورحمة.

## The fourteenth canon:
### a Christian is not to become a soldier

It is not fitting[60] that a Christian should become a soldier unless a chief with a sword compels him. The sin of blood shall not be charged to him,[61] but if he sheds blood he should not participate in the mysteries unless he has been purified by chastisement, weeping and wailing. He should not approach with duplicity but in the fear of God.

## The fifteenth canon:
### a number of acts which should not be performed

A fornicator, or somebody who lives off immoral earnings, or an effeminate, especially one who talks filth, or a beggar,[62] or a degenerate (ἄσωτος), or a sorcerer, or an astrologer, or a soothsayer, or an interpreter of dreams, or a snake-charmer,[63] or a rabble-rouser, or somebody who manufactures phylacteries (φυλακτήρια), or an usurer, or an exploiter, or anyone who loves the world,[64] or anyone who loves oaths, that is swearing, or a misanthrope, or a hypocrite, or somebody who slanders people, or somebody who determines whether the hours and days are propitious: do not catechize any of these, or any like them, and do not baptize them, unless they renounce all suchlike activities, and unless three witnesses testify on their account that they have indeed renounced all such vices, because often it is the case that people continue in their tendencies into their old age, unless they are empowered with a mighty strengthening.

And if, after baptism, they are found to be continuing in these vices they are so to be excluded from the church until they repent with tears, and fasting, and acts of charity.

---

60 Literally "it does not go." As Coquin notes, this is an over-literal translation of the Coptic ϣϣⲉ.
61 Coquin suggests that the process of translation may have confused the text, and that originally it read along the lines of: "It is not fitting that a Christian should become a soldier unless he is compelled. The sin of blood shall not be charged to a chief with a sword..." If this is the case then the "chief with a sword" may be a governor invested with the *ius gladii*, as explained by Ulpian *apud Digesta* 1.18.6.8.
62 Literally, somebody who is weak or disabled. Coquin translates as "désoeuvré", and is followed by Bebawi (in Bradshaw), "idler." Oddly Coquin suggests λῶταξ as the underlying Greek.
63 The translation is not assured. Possibly some other form of magic is intended. The corresponding phrase in *Traditio apostolica* is obscure, and offers no assistance.
64 A literal translation, though this may represent a misunderstanding of φιλόκοσμος, as in *Can. Hipp.* 38, n. 200 below, and refer to somebody who loves ornament.

القانون السادس عشر
لاجل نصراني له سرية ويتزوج عليها
نصراني تكون له سرية لا سيما وقد رزقت معه ولدا اذا تزوج عليها فانه قاتل الانسان الا ان يجدها في زناء.

## The sixteenth canon:
### concerning a Christian who has a concubine and marries other than her

A Christian who has a concubine and marries other than her, especially if she has borne a child by him, is to be reckoned a homicide, unless he discovers her in fornication.[65]

---

[65] Cf. *Sent. Conc. Nic.* 7.1: "A man (δέ) who fornicates (πορνεύειν), whilst having a wife, is worthless, and an infanticide." Achelis, *Ältesten Quellen*, 167, explains this as seeing him as committing a sin such that he should be treated as a murderer. This attitude is to be contrasted to that manifested in the west; in a context in which concubinage was common, and in which it was common for men to leave concubines, even when they had children, in order to marry advantageously (the most well-known example being that of Augustine) Leo I (*Ep.* 167, *inquisitio* 4) defends such a practice as right, normal, and sanctioned by Scripture. For discussion, see Reynolds, *Marriage in the western church*, 162-167.

## القانون السابع عشر

### لاجل الامرأة الحرة وما تفعله

امرأة حرة لا تعطي وارس عليها في الكنيسة ولا انها سنه عرسها ولا تدع شعرها محلولا اي يكون ضغائر عليها في بيت الله ولا تلبس ذوائب على رأسها وهي تريد تتناول من السرائر المقدسة ولا تعطي اولادها التي تلدهم للدايات بل تربيهم هي وحدها كأسم الزيجة ولا تتوانى عن خدمة بيتها ولا تجواب بعلها في شيء وان كانت تعرف اكثر منه بل تذكر الله في كل وقت وتعرف اكثر مع الذكور ولا تظهر لاحد من الناس بل تكن تخدم بعلها كسيد. وتهتم بالفقراء القريبين منها وتهتم بابكار القرابين عوضا من عالم فارغ

# The seventeenth canon: concerning a free woman and what she should do

A free woman should not wear jewels in church,[66] not even in the year of her marriage.[67] Nor should her hair be unbound, that is to say in plaits,[68] in the house of God. Nor should she wear braids on her head when she wishes to participate in the holy mysteries. And she should not give her children, those whom she has borne, to wet-nurses, but should raise them in accordance with the law of marriage.[69] And she should not be slack with regard to her housework, nor should she answer back to her husband in anything, even if she knows more than he, but should remember God at all times. Even if she knows more than men she should not let this be known, but should serve her husband like a lord. She should care for the poor nearby, she should concern herself with the offerings of first-fruits rather than with vain decoration,[70]

---

66  The text reads "shall not give dark-yellow". The word "give" may be explained with reference to Coptic † (give) which with the prepositions ϩⲓⲱⲱ or ⲉⲣⲟ might mean "wear." The question is that of what is worn. A possibility canvassed by Coquin is that this refers to the *flammeum*, or wedding veil, known in Roman times. Literary evidence (Catullus *Carm.* 61.8–10, 68.133; Lucan *Pharsalia* 2.360–364; Pliny *Nat. Hist.* 21.46) and material remains indicate that this was an orange-yellow colour (see DiLuzio, *A place at the altar*, 40–41). However, rightly in this translator's opinion, he prefers to see it as a rendition of the Coptic ⲛⲟⲩⲃ (gold), which might be an adjective as well as a noun, intended to render χρυσία. Coquin notes the link with 1 Tim 2:9–12 and 1 Pet 3:3, in addition to which we may cite *Sent. Conc. Nic.* 4.3: "A woman who dresses herself in gold just (μάλιστα) as she goes to church (ἐκκλησία) shows herself to be like a worshipper of idols (εἴδωλον).

67  This phrase is also puzzling. "Not even in the year of her marriage" is one possible reading of the Arabic, but "even if it is a custom sanctioned by her husband" (so Bebawi [in Bradshaw], following Coquin; the same interpretation is lent by Haneberg) is also possible; the reading depends entirely on the vocalization. There is no parallel which give guidance. "Not in the year of her marriage" might refer, as Coquin notes, to the *flammeum*, and thus to give weight to that interpretation, though we may suggest that it refers to jewellery obtained as part of a dowry (such being commonly found in Egypt) (see, for examples, references to such a custom in P.Mich. 434, P.Oxy. 267, P.Oxy. 905, P.Oxy. 795, P.Mil.Vogl. 85, all from Egypt and from the imperial period.) As such it may reasonably refer back to jewellery, and so the second understanding of the phrase is preferred. Readers may choose to differ.

68  Cf., again, *Sent. Conc. Nic.* 4.5: "Any woman who wears (φέρειν) jewellery on her head is making a display of her stupidity, and whatever woman wears her hair loosened, that it to say in ringlets, is sending out an invitation (καλεῖν) to the senseless." Coquin explains the apparent contradiction with reference to a possible confusion by the translator of two Coptic words.

69  Literally "in accordance with the name of marriage." Coquin postulates that there has been confusion between νόμος and ὄμοια. We may note that wet-nurses were widely used in elite circles in antiquity. See, for references, my article "Milch", 784–803.

70  Literally: "with a vain world." κόσμος has been misunderstood by the Coptic translator.

لانك لاتجد واحدة تحلي باحجار جواهر حسنة مثل واحدة حسنة في طبيعتها وحدها وجودتها مثل هذه. هذا يجعلوه لهن رقيبا ان يكن نظافا ولا يكن محبات للذة ولا يكن ذوات ضحك ولا يتكلمن جملة في الكنيسة لان بيت الله ما هو موضع كلام بل موضع صلاة بخوف. الذي يتكلم في الكنيسة يخرج ولا يتقرب في تلك الدفعة من السرائر.

والمتعظ الذي يستحق النور لا يمنعه الوقت لان مثاله بينة ومعلم الكنيسة هو الذي يحكم بهذا الفعل.

### القانون الثامن عشر

لاجل القوابل وانعزال النساء عن الرجال في الصلاة والعذارى يغطين رؤوسهن ولاجل النساء اللاتي يلدن

ومن بعد ما يفرغ المعلم معا يعلم كل يوم فليصلوا وهم متفرقون من النصارى.

for you will not find a woman adorned with precious gems as beautiful as one like this, whose beauty is in her nature alone, and in her excellence. This should make them careful[71] to be pure, and not pleasure loving, not being prone to laughter, and not to say a word in church, for it is the house of God; it is not a place for conversation, but a place for prayer in fearfulness. Anyone[72] who speaks in church should be expelled, and is not to approach the mysteries on that occasion.[73]

A catechumen who is worthy of the light[74] should not be prevented on the basis of time, for his conduct is the evidence. It is the teacher of the church who is to be the judge in this matter.

The eighteenth canon:
concerning midwives[75] and the segregation of women from men at prayer; that virgins should cover their heads; and concerning women who have given birth[76]

They (the catechumens) should pray each day, when the teacher has finished instruction, separately from the Christians.

---

71  Literally: "Thus they are made into a guard..." An over-literal translation of the Coptic.
72  As Coquin points out, the pronoun here is masculine. However, since Coptic relative pronouns are not gendered, the Greek original might have been feminine.
73  Cf. *Sent. Conc. Nic.* 3.2: Anyone who speaks in church, especially (μάλιστα) during reading, is abusing God.
74  Riedel suggests that this represents φωτισμός.
75  Whereas the word here may mean somebody who is pregnant (so Haneberg), Riedel points out that such a meaning is not possible here.
76  There is some variation among the witnesses regarding the division of canons around here. Following Coquin, the division and title here are as given in R.

والنساء القوابل لا يتناولن من السرائر الا بعد ان يتطهرن اولا وطهارتهن تكون من هذا فان كان المولود الذي قبلنه ذكرا فعشرين يوما وإن كانت انثى فاربعين يوما. ولا يدعن النفاس بل يصلين الله على التي قبلت. واذا مضت الى بيت الله من قبل ان تتطهر فلتصلي مع المتعظين الذين لم يقبلوا بعد ولا استحقوا الخلطة.

والنساء يكن منعزلات في موضع لا يقبلن ذكرا جملة.

ويضع المعلم يده على المتعظين قبل ان يصرفهم.

والعذارى النساء اذا كملت درجة شبابهن فليغطين رؤوسهن مثل النساء الكبائر ببلاليهن ليس بثوب خفيف.

الامراة التي تلد فلتنقم خارجا عن الموضع المقدس اربعين يوما ان كان الولد الذي ولدته ذكرا وان كانت انثى فثمانين يوما. واذا دخلت الكنيسة تصلي مع المتعظين.

والقوابل فليكن كثيرا لئلا يكن خارجا كل ايام حياتهن.

The midwives should not participate in the mysteries until they have been purified;[77] their purification is thus. Twenty days if the child they have delivered is male, forty days if she is female.[78] They should not neglect those who are lying-in,[79] but should pray to God for those who are lying-in. If she goes to the house of God before she is purified she should pray with the catechumens who have not yet been received and who have not yet been considered deserving of incorporation.

Women are to be segregated in a place, and are not to kiss any man.

Before he dismisses them, the teacher lays his hand on the catechumens.

Virgins who have completed the degree of their girlhood should cover their heads like grown women, with their shawls (παλλίον), not a skimpy veil.

A woman who has given birth should stay away from the sacred place for forty days if the child she has borne is male, and twenty-four days if she is female.[80] If she enters the church she should pray with the catechumens.

There should be many midwives, so that they are not excluded for their entire lives.[81]

---

77 A good insight into ancient midwifery is given through Soranus *Gyn.* 1. In particular *Gyn.* 1.3-4 is interesting in establishing ethical criteria for midwives, who should be literate, alert, hard-working and respectable. However, the inscriptional evidence indicates that midwives were largely of the freedperson class. See Buonopane, "Medicae nell'occidente romano" (though this concentrates on western evidence).
78 Given the distinction here between the periods of absence for a midwife and for a mother, we must wonder whether some corruption has entered the text, and that the periods of absence should be the same as for a mother.
79 Or "the time of lying in."
80 Lev 12.1-5. What is intriguing in this canon is that the provision is extended to the midwives. It is possible that the provision originated in the duty of the midwife to give perinatal care, as Soranus describes. Hence it is said that the midwives should not neglect those lying in.
81 Coquin reads *a'n ḥayātunna* (for their lives) the reading of R, here whereas m reads *kullan ḥayātunna* (all their lives). Rifaat Ebied conjectures a reading of *kullan āyām ḥayātunna* (all the days of their lives.)

## القانون التاسع عشر

لاجل متعظ يقيل على استشهاد قبل المعمودية يدفن مع الشهداء ولاجل المتعظين والشروط التي يعملها المتعظون عند المعمودية واستحلاف وترتيب قداس المعمودية وتقديس قداس الجسد والدم

اذا ضبطوا متعظا للاستشهاد ويقتل من قبل ان يتعمد فليدفن مع الشهداء كلهم لانه قد تعمد بدمه وحده.

### فصل المتعظين

المتعظ اذا عمد وشهد له من جهة من ياتي به انه سعى في الوصايا في الزمان الذي اتعظ فيه ان كان عاد المرضى او دفع للعاجزين وحفظ نفسه من كل كلام رديء سمج وهل بغض المجد الفارغ وازدرى بالكبرياء واصطفى له التواضع ويعترف للاسقف ان وزره عليه وحده لكي يرتضيه الاسقف ويثمنه على السرائر. وانه صار نظيفا بحق وحينئذ يقرأ عليه الانجيل في ذلك الوقت ويسأل دفعات كثيرة هل انت ذو قلبين او يضطرك سبب او حشمة لانه لا يسخر احد بملكوت السموات بل يدفع لمحبيها من كل قلوبهم.

والذين يتعمدون يستحموا بالماء يوم الخميس من الاسبوع ويأكلوا ويصوموا الجمعة وإن كانت هي امراة ويتفق ان يلحقها الطمث فلا تتعمد في تلك الدفعة بل تتأخر الى ان تطهر.

وفي يوم السبت يجمع الاسقف الذين يتعمدون ويدعهم يحنون رؤوسهم الى الشرق ويفرش يده عليهم. ويصلي ويطرد عنهم كل روح خبيث في اكسرجسمسه وهم ايضا لا يعودون اليهم من الآن بفعالهم.

## The nineteenth canon:
### concerning a catechumen killed on account of his confession before baptism, that he is buried with the martyrs: and concerning the catechumens and the qualifications that they fulfil during baptism and the exorcism and the ordering of the liturgy of baptism and the consecratory liturgy of the Body and the Blood

If a catechumen is apprehended for bearing witness, and is killed before baptism, he is to be buried among all the martyrs, for he has indeed been baptized in his blood.

### Chapter of the catechumens

A catechumen, when he is baptized, and the one who bears witness for him, by whom he is presented, that he strove in the commandments during the period of his catechumenate, that he visited the sick, or gave to the helpless, and kept himself away from any evil and disgusting word, and has hated false glory, despised pride, and chosen humility for himself, confessing to the bishop that he alone is responsible for himself, so that the bishop is satisfied and reckons him (worthy) of the mysteries. If he has in truth become pure he reads the Gospel over him at that time, and asks frequently "Are you in two minds,[82] or are you forced for any reason, or from convention? Because nobody mocks the Kingdom of the heavens, but it is given to those who love it with all their hearts."

Those who are to be baptized should bathe in water on the fifth day of the week, and eat, and should fast on the Friday. And if there is a woman, and it so happens that she is menstruating, she is not to be baptized on that occasion but should wait until she has been purified.[83]

And on the seventh day of the week the bishop shall gather those who are to be baptized; he shall make them bow their heads towards the east and lay his hand upon them. He shall pray and expel every evil spirit from them by his exorcism (ἐξορκισμός). They shall not return to them thenceforth through what they do.

---

82   Literally "of two hearts." A Copticism reflecting the common use of the term δίψυχος and its cognates in the church order tradition.

83   As Coquin points out, all these provision tend to exclude the possibility that paschal baptism is intended. Not too much significance should be read into this, however, and in particular this should not be taken as evidence of an Alexandrian origin to the *Canones*. As Bradshaw,· "'Diem baptismo sollemniorem'", 137–47, points out, not only is the range of evidence for paschal baptism very limited, but (here at 145) Cappadocian practice was certainly not to restrict baptism to Easter.

فاذا فرغ مما يستحلفهم ينفخ في وجوههم ويرشم صدورهم وجباههم واسماعهم وانوفهم. ويكونوا ساهرين كل ليلتهم في الكلام المقدس والصلوات.

ويقاموا عند صياح الديك على الماء ماء بحر بتيار صاف مستعد مقدس.

والذين يتكلمون عن الاطفال الصغار يعروهم من ثيابهم في الاول والذين هم قادرون ان يكفلوهم وحدهم ومن بعد النساء يكن اخرهم كلهم ليعرينهن من ثيابهن وينحين حليهن ذهبا كان او غيره ويحللن شعور رؤوسهن لئلا ينزل معهن شيء من الارواح الغريبة الى ماء الميلاد الثاني. وينحين

والاسقف يصلي على زيت الاستحلاف ويدفعه لقسيس ويصلي على زيت المسحة الذي هو زيت الشكر ويدفعه لقسيس اخر والذي يمسك زيت الاستحلاف يقف على يسار الاسقف والذي يمسك زيت المسحة يقف على يمين الاسقف.

والذي يعمدوا يحول وجهه الى الغرب ويقول هكذا اني أجحدك يا ابليس وكل خدمتك. فاذا قال هكذا يدهنه القسيس بزيت الاستحلاف الذي صلي عليه ان تزول عنه كل روح خبيثة. ويدفع للقسيس الذي على الماء من جهة شماس. ويمسك قسيس يده اليمين ويحول وجهه الى الشرق على الماء. ومن قبل ان ينزل الى الماء ووجهه الى الشرق وهو قائم على الماء يقول هكذا من بعد ما نال زيت الاستحلاف اني أؤمن وانحني لك ولخدمتك كلها ايها الاب والابن والروح القدس.

وهكذا ينزل الى المياه.

When he has finished adjuring them he breathes on their faces, and marks their chests, their foreheads, their ears, and their noses. They are to spend all their night in the holy word and in prayers.

At cockcrow they stand by the water, the pure water running into a vessel, prepared and sanctified.[84]

Those who are to speak on behalf of the small children remove the clothes from them first of all, then those who are able to make answer on their own behalf. After this the women remove their clothes, last of all. They remove their jewellery, whether of gold or anything else, and loosen the hairs of their heads, so that nothing which is of an alien spirit[85] should go down with them into the water of second birth.

And the bishop prays over the oil of exorcism and passes it to a presbyter, and he prays over the oil of chrism, that is the oil of thanksgiving, and hands to another presbyter. The one who holds the oil of exorcism stands to the left of the bishop, and the one who holds the oil of chrism stands to the right of the bishop.

The one being baptized turns his face towards the west and says: "I renounce you, Satan, and your service entirely." And when he says this the presbyter anoints him with the oil of exorcism, over which prayer was said, so that every evil spirit might depart from him. He is passed to the presbyter by the water by a deacon. A presbyter takes his right hand and turns his face towards the east, near the water. Before he goes down to the water, his face towards the east, while he is standing by the water, he says this, after receiving the oil of exorcism: "I believe,[86] and I submit[87] to you, and to your service entirely, O Father, Son, and Holy Spirit."

And so he goes down into the waters.

---

84  The phrase is not altogether clear, not the least because of the range of meanings of *baḥr*, which may mean any body of water, here rendered "vessel", but capable of meaning "sea" or "river". Burkitt, "The baptismal rite", 279, n. suggests "by the water, a running stream, pure, prepared and holy." Coquin suggests a Coptic *Vorlage* of ⲉⲓⲟⲙ.
85  R reads "evil spirit."
86  *āʾwʾmin*, which, as Coquin suggests, renders ⲧⲛⲁϩⲧⲉ, in both languages conveying the idea of trust as much as belief.
87  *ānḥany*, literally meaning "I incline myself." As Coquin states, this represents ⲭⲛⲉ ⲭⲱ= (to bow one's head) the standard rendition of ὑποτάσσομαι.

ويضع القسيس يده على رأسه ويسأله ويقول أتؤمن بالله الاب ضابط الكل؟ والذي يتعمد يقول اني اؤمن. فيغطسه في الماء دفعة ويده على رأسه. ويسأله ثاني دفعة ويقول له أتؤمن بيسوع المسيح ابن الله الذي ولدته مريم العذراء من روح القدس الذي أتي لاجل خلاص البشر الذي صلب على عهد بيلاطس البنطي الذي مات وقام من الموتى في اليوم الثالث وصعد الى السموات وجلس عن يمين الاب ويأتي يدين الاحياء والاموات؟ فيقول اني اؤمن فيغطسه في الماء ثاني دفعة. ويسأله ثالث دفعة ويقول له أتؤمن بالروح القدس البارقليط الفائض من الاب والابن؟ فاذا قال اني أؤمن غطسه ثالث دفعة في الماء. ويقول كل دفعة اني اعمدك باسم الاب والابن والروح القدس الثالوث المتساوية.

ويصعد من الماء ويأخد القسيس دهن الاوخارسدية ويصلب على جبهته وفمه وصدره ويمسح كل جسده ورأسه ووجهه قائلا اني امسحك باسم الاب والابن والروح القدس ويمسحه بثوب ويحفظه له ويلبسه ثيابه ويدخل به الى الكنيسة.

ويضع الاسقف يده على المتعمدين كلهم ويصلي هكذا ويقول نباركك يا رب يا الله ضابط الكل لانك جعلت هؤلاء مستحقين ان يولدوا دفعة أخرى وتفيض روحك القدس عليهم ويكونوا واحدا وحيدا في جسد الكنيسة وليس هم مفترقين بافعال غريبة بل كما وهبت لهم غفران خطاياهم هب لهم ايضا عاربون ملكوتك بسيدنا يسوع المسيح هذا الذي من جهته المجد لك معه والروح القدس الى ابد الابدين. آمين.

The presbyter places his hand upon his head and asks him: "Do you believe in God the Father almighty?" And the one being baptized responds: "I believe." So he plunges him once into the water, with his hand on his head. And he asks him a second time, and says to him, "Do you believe in Jesus Christ the Son of God, who was born of the Virgin Mary by the Holy Spirit, who came for the salvation of humanity,[88] who was crucified during the period of Pontius Pilate, who died and rose from the dead on the third day, and ascended into the heavens, and sat at the right hand of the Father, and will come to judge the living and the dead?" As he says "I believe" he plunges him into the water a second time. And he asks him a third time, and says to him; "Do you believe in the Holy Spirit the paraklete (παράκλητος) who flows from the Father and the Son?"[89] And as he says "I believe" he plunges him a third time into the water. And each time he says "I baptize you in the name of the Father, and of the Son, and of the Holy Spirit, the equal Trinity."

And he ascends from the water, and the presbyter takes the oil of thanksgiving (εὐχαριστία) signs the cross on his forehead, his mouth, his chest, and wipes his entire body, saying: "I anoint you in the name of the Father, and of the Son, and of the Holy Spirit." The presbyter wipes him with a cloth which he keeps for him,[90] he dresses him in his clothes, and takes him into the church.

The bishop lays his hand on all those who have been baptized and prays thus, saying: "We bless you, all powerful Lord God, you have made these worthy of a second birth, and have poured out your Holy Spirit upon them, so they shall be one in the body of the church alone, not to be removed by any alien deeds: but as you have endowed them with the forgiveness of their sins, endow them also with the pledge (ἀρραβών) of your Kingdom.[91] Through Our Lord Jesus Christ, through whom be the glory to you, with him and the Holy Spirit, to the ages of ages. Amen.

---

88  As Bradshaw observes, the purpose of the incarnation is not found within the creed of *Traditio apostolica* but is found in a number of fourth-century creeds.
89  On the meaning of this phrase see the introduction 6.2. Achelis, *Ältesten Quellen*, 217, suggested that this phrase was an interpolation, though Riedel reasonably asks whether this is an interpolation that a Copt would be likely to make.
90  Coquin notes that R has an additional word here, *malkma*, which he reasonably suggests might be a corrupted transliteration of κάλυμμα. Possibly this was a scribal annotation which has entered the text.
91  Cf. 2 Cor. 1:22 (God has anointed us and signed [σφραγισάμενος] us, giving us the Spirit as an ἀρραβών.)

وبعد ذلك يصلب على جباههم بزيت المسحة ويقبلهم قائلا الرب معكم.

ويقول ايضا الذين يعمدوا ومع روحك.

هكذا يفعل بالواحد الذي يتعمد.

ومن بعد ذلك يصلون مع الشعب كله المؤمنين ويقبلوهم ويفرحون معهم بتهليل.

وبعد ذلك الشماس يبدأ يقدس والاسقف يكمل اوخارسدية الجسد والدم الذي الرب. وادا فرغ يناول الشعب وهو قائم على مائدة جسد ودم الرب والقساء حاملو كأسات دم المسيح وكأسات أخر لبن وعسل لكي يعلموا الذين يتناولون انهم ولدوا دفعة أخرى بصغر لان الصغار يتناولون اللبن والعسل. واذا لم يكن ثم قساء ليحملوا هولاء فليحملهم الشمامسة.

وهكذا يدفع لهم الاسقف من جسد المسيح ويقول هذا جسد المسيح فيقولون هم أمين.

والذي يدفع لهم من الكأس يقول هذا هو دم المسيح فيقولون آمين.

And after that he makes the sign of the cross on their foreheads with the oil of chrism,[92] and he kisses them and says: "The Lord be with you." And those who are baptized answer likewise: "And with your spirit." And he does the same with all who have been baptized.

And thereafter they pray with all the faithful people, they kiss them, and rejoice with them in acclamations.

After this the deacon begins the liturgy,[93] and the bishop completes the Eucharist (εὐχαριστία) of the body and blood of the Lord. When it is finished he gives communion to the people, standing by the table of the body and blood of the Lord. The presbyters hold the cups of the blood of the Lord, and the other cups, of milk and honey, so that those who communicate might know that they are born again, like infants, as infants partake of milk and honey. And if there are no presbyters to carry them, the deacons carry them.

And so the bishop gives them the body of Christ, and says: "This is the body of Christ." So they reply: "Amen."

And the one who gives them the cup says "this is the blood of Christ." So they reply: "Amen."

---

92  Such is the reading of R (*bizeyti almashati*) cf. the reading of m: "with the sign of love" (*birušmi almaḥbati*). Hanssens, "L'édition critique", 512–513, prefers this reading. First he suggests that whichever line of transmission made the alteration, it is a deliberate act. Thus he suggests that it is more likely that a scribe would alter the reading to conform it to the practice, namely anointing, with which he is familiar. Against this, however, we may suggest that a scribe so intent in making alterations would also omit the prior presbyteral anointing. Hanssens also suggests that there is support in *Testamentum Domini* 2.9 where, he suggests, the oil is not employed in this consignation. Here he is mistaken, for although the consignation is made without oil, it is immediately preceded by the same anointing which we find here in the *Canones*, as it is in the Latin and Axumite Ethiopic versions of *Traditio apostolica*, and thus may be seen as a consignation in the oil with which the candidate has already been anointed. It seems that the redactor has here combined the episcopal anointing with the consignation, by omitting the prayer said at the anointing. We may thus see that the scribe of m might be confused through the omission of the prayer and so substitute the sign of peace for the anointing at the consignation. As noted in the introduction, it is probable that the redactor did not know of any second post-baptismal anointing; such indeed is a peculiarity of *Traditio apostolica*. However, it is also possible that the redactor knew of a post-baptismal consignation with oil, and thus has effected the combination of rites.

93  Literally, "begins to consecrate." Coquin suggests that there is confusion because the text originally employed the word ἀναφέρειν. The import had been that the deacon brought the gifts, which is taken to mean that he offers them.

ومن بعد يتناولون من اللبن والعسل لتذكار الدهر الأتي ومدحوا الخيرات التي فيه هذا الذي لا يعود الى مرارة ولا يضمحلوا.

وهكذا صاروا نصارى كاملين وغذوهم بجسد المسيح ويحاربون بحكمة لتنور سيرتهم في الفضائل لا قدام بعضهم بعض بل أمام الامم ايضا حتى انهم يحسدوهم ويتنصروا ويروا نمو الذين انيروا انها عالية وافضل من عادات الناس.

فاما الذين تعمدوا والاخر الذين صاموا معهم فلا يذوقوا شيئا من قبل ان يتناولوا من جسد المسيح لانه لا يعد لهم صوما بل خطيئة. والذي يذوق شيئا من قبل ان يتناول الجسد فانه يخالف ويزدري بالله. فاذا كمل القداس له السلطان ان يأكل ما احب.

وليجتمع جميع المتعظمين بعضهم مع بعض وليكفهم معلم واحد يعلمهم بكفاف ويصلوا ويحنوا ركبهم. وهم لا يذوقوا شيئا من قبل ان يفرغوا الذين تعمدوا معا يتناولون الجسد والدم.

## القانون العشرون
### لاجل صوم الاربعاء والجمعة والاربعين

في ايام الصوم التي بنيت الاربعاء والجمعة والاربعون والذي يزيد على هذا فانه ينال اجرا ومن خالف هذا من غير مرض او شدة او ضرورة فهو خارج عن القانون وهو مخالف لله الذي صام عنا.

And after this they communicate with the milk and honey, to commemorate the age to come, and the sweetness of its good things, which will not return to bitterness and will not decay.⁹⁴

So they become complete Christians, nourished by the body of Christ, struggling in wisdom so that their lives may shine with virtues, not only before each other but before the nations, such that they might envy them,⁹⁵ that they may become Christians, and see that the progress of those who are illuminated is great, and that their behaviour is more virtuous than the manners of the peoples.

Those who have been baptized, and also those who fast with them, are not to taste anything before they partake of the body of Christ, otherwise it will not be reckoned a fast but a failing. Anyone who tastes anything before communicating in the body is disobeying and disdaining God. When the liturgy is over he can⁹⁶ eat whatever he wishes.⁹⁷

The catechumens should all gather together, and one teacher is sufficient to instruct them all adequately. They should pray and bend the knee. Those who are being baptized are not to taste anything before they have finished communicating in the body and the blood.

The twentieth canon:
concerning the fast of Wednesday, and Friday, and Lent⁹⁸

The fasting days which are established⁹⁹ are the Wednesday, the Friday, and Lent. Whoever augments these will be so rewarded, and whoever transgresses them, except in sickness, constraint, or necessity, is outside the rule (κανών) and is disobeying God, who fasted for us.

---

94  Literally "disappear."
95  Coquin persuasively suggests that the Arabic here represents ⲕⲱϩ, which in turn represents ζηλοῦν, which might mean either "envy" or "imitate", and that the second meaning was that originally intended.
96  Literally, "the power is for him", another Copticism, rendering ⲟⲩⲛ̄ ϭⲟⲙ ⲙ̄ⲙⲟϥ.
97  Cf. the statement of Dionysius of Alexandria Ad Basileiden 1, that the paschal fast should not be concluded before midnight.
98  Literally, "the forty."
99  Literally "built." Coquin notes that ⲕⲱⲧ might be used in the sense of fixing a law.

ويرسل من جهة الاسقف للموعوظين خبز قد طهر بالصلاة فينالوا شركة الكنيسة.

### القانون الحادي والعشرون

لاجل اجتماع جميع الكهنه والشعب الى الكنيسة كل يوم

القساء يجتمعوا في كل يوم الى الكنيسة والشمامسة والابودياقنيون والاغنستسيون وكل الشعب وقت يسقع الديك ويصنعون الصلاة والمزامير وقراءة الكتب والصلوات كوصية الرسول القائل التفت الى القراءة الى ان احضر. والذي يتأخر عن الاكليرس من غير مرض ولم يتورب فليفرق.

والاخر المرضى هو شفاء لهم المضي الى الكنيسة لينالوا من ماء الصلاة وزيت الصلاة. الا ان يكون المريض مدنفا هاويا يعوده الاكليرس كل يوم الذين يعرفونه.

Bread, purified by means of prayer, shall be sent to the catechumens by the bishop, so that they can participate in the companionship of the church.

## The twenty-first canon:
### concerning the daily gathering of the assembled priesthood and the congregation in the church

The presbyters gather every day at the church, as do the deacons, the subdeacons (ὑποδιάκων), the readers (ἀναγνώστης), and all the congregation, at the time when the cock crows. They are to take up prayers, and psalms, and reading of Scripture, and the prayer, in accordance with the direction of the apostle, who said "Attend to reading until I return."[100] Anyone who follows the clergy (κλῆρος) in and does not hasten, except in illness, is to be excluded.[101]

Those who are sick will also[102] find healing for themselves in coming to church, to receive the water of prayer and the oil of prayer,[103] unless he is gravely ill and close to death. The clergy (κλῆρος) who know him should visit daily.[104]

---

100  1 Tim 4:13.
101  Cf. *Sent. Conc. Nic.* 8.14: "Anyone who hurries to church receives a double blessing; anyone who is late except of (χωρίς) necessity (ἀνάγκη) is too late to be blessed." This is the reading of R; d and m both read "any of the clergy" for "follows the clergy", and turn the canon in various ways into a discussion of clergy who are less than enthusiastic about the daily gathering.
102  Literally "the other sick will". A mistranslation of Coptic ⲕⲉ, which might mean both "also" and "other."
103  Probably εὐχέλαιον, a term which, as Malvy, "L'onction des malades", 223, points out, is in contemporary usage.
104  This is the direct translation of the Arabic. One wonders whether the sentence should read: "If he is gravely ill and close to death the clergy who know him should visit daily." This canon is paraphrased in the *Nomocanon* of Ibn al Assal (9.24), and such is Ibn al Assal's understanding. It is hard to account for the error; the issue is with the first Arabic words, *ālā ān*, which mean "unless." If, however, the text simply read *ān* then this might mean "if." Is it possible that the Coptic, following Greek, read ⲁⲗⲗⲁ, which has been carelessly transliterated as *ālā*? The error would be assisted by the fact that the protasis of such a conditional in Coptic is a separate clause, so might be read with the preceding rather than the following clause.

### القانون الثاني والعشرون

لاجل الاسبوع الذي للفصح الذي لليهود يتجنب فيه الفرح ولاجل ما يؤكل فيه ولاجل من كان في غربة ولم يعرف البسخة

والاسبوع الذي للفصح الذي لليهود فليتحفظ فيه كل الشعب بتحفظ كثير ليصوموا عن كل شهوة فيه حتى الى كلمة لا يقولوها بفرح بل بحزن عارفين ان رب الكل الغير متألم تألم عنا فيه لكي بصبر الالام لنخرج عن الالم الذي نستحقه لاجل آثامنا ونحن ايضا نشارك الالم الذي قبله عنا لنشاركه في ملكوته.

والطعام الذي في البسخة خبز وملح وحده وماء.

وان كان واحد مريضا او في كورة ليس فيها نصراني ويفرغ زمان البسخة ولم يعرفه كحده او لاجل مرض الاخر فليصوموا بعد الخمسين ويصنعوا البصخة بادب. لتتبين سريرتهم انهم لم يتوانوا بغير خوف ليس يصومون انهم يصنعون بسخة وحودهم ليصنعوا اساسا اخرا غير الذي هو موضوع.

The twenty-second canon:
concerning the week of the Passover of the Jews, during which joyousness is waived, and concerning what is eaten then, and concerning somebody who is abroad and does not know about the pascha (πάσχα)[105]

During the week of the Passover, which is for the Jews, the entire congregation should be watchful with great vigilance. During it they are to fast from every pleasure; not even a word should be spoken with joy during it, but with sadness, knowing that the Lord of all, who is impassible, suffered on our behalf, so that by his patience in suffering we might escape the suffering which we merit on account of our sins. We too participate in the suffering which he accepted for us so that with him we might participate in his Kingdom.[106]

Food, for the duration of the Pascha (πάσχα), is bread and salt only, and water.

And if somebody is sick or in a place where there is no Christian, and the period of the Pascha (πάσχα) comes to an end, and he did not know it owing to his solitude, or on account of illness, they are to fast after the Pentecost,[107] and they are to observe the Pascha (πάσχα) with discipline. Their intent[108] should be clear; they are not late through lack of reverence, and they are not fasting and observing Pascha (πάσχα) on their own to give a foundation to anything other than that which is set in place.[109]

---

105 Two words are used for Pascha in this chapter, reflecting Coptic usage. *Faṣḥ*, derived from Syriac, indicates the day, whereas *baskha* indicates the week known now as "Great week" or "Holy Week".
106 2 Tim 2:12; Rom 8:17; Phil 3:10-11; 1 Pet 4:13.
107 Literally "the fifty."
108 Reading *sarayratuhum* with the MSS. Riedel conjectures *šadiydatuhum*, "their intensity" or "their seriousness."
109 Coquin suggests an allusion here to 1 Cor 3:11.

## القانون الثالث والعشرون

لاجل التعليم انه اعظم من البحر ويجب السعي في طلبه

واخوتنا الاساقفة رتبوا اشياء في مدنهم كاوامر ابهاتنا الرسل مما لم نقدر نذكرهم لنقص خدمتنا. فلا يغيرهم من ياتي بعدنا لانه قال لاجل التعليم انه اعظم من البحر. وليس له انتهاء ولاجل هذا نحن نسعى في طلب التعليم بكل مثال فلنقبله اذا وجدناه.


## القانون الرابع والعشرون

لاجل افتقاد الاسقف للمرضى واذا صلى مريض في كنيسة وله بيت فليمضي اليه

يكن شماس يمشي مع الاسقف في كل وقت ليعرفه فعل كل احد ولاجل واحد مريض ليعرفه به لانه كثير للمريض ان يفتقده مقدم الكهنة. ويكون يهدأ من مرضه اذا مضى اليه الاسقف ولا سيما اذا صلى عليه لان ظل بطرس اشفى المرضى الا ان يكون قد فرغ اجله.

لم يجعل المرضى يناموا في الكيميدارين بل الفقراء فلاجل هذا الذي له بيت اذا مرض لا ينقل في بيت الله بل يصلي له غير ويعود الى بيته.

The twenty-third canon:
concerning knowledge, that it is greater than the sea, and that one should be eager in its pursuit

Our brothers, the bishops, have ordered matters in their cities in accordance with the directions of our fathers, the apostles. We have been unable to mention them due to the inadequacy of our work. Nobody coming after us should alter them, since it is said concerning knowledge that it is greater than the sea.[110] On this account we are eager[111] in the pursuit of knowledge in every way; let us accept it when we find it.

The twenty-fourth canon:
concerning the bishop's visitation to the sick, and when a sick person has prayed in a church, and has a home, that he should go there

There should be a deacon accompanying[112] the bishop at all times, so that he may inform him regarding every matter. He is to inform him concerning anyone who is sick, since it is a matter of importance for the sick person if the chief of the priests visits him. It eases his sickness if the bishop comes to him, especially when he prays over him,[113] for the shadow of Peter healed the sick,[114] as long as he has not completed his appointed time.

The sick are not to sleep in the dormitory[115] (κοιμητήριον) but rather the poor. For this reason, any sick person who has a house is not carried into the house of God except only to pray, and then to return to his home.

---

110 Isa 11:19.
111 Or, if Coquin's suggestion of a badly rendered Coptic optative is accepted, "Let us be eager...".
112 Literally, "walking with." The original Greek, reflected by the Sahidic version of *Traditio apostolica*, was almost certainly a form of προσκαρτερέω; it is possible that the Sahidic translator of the *Canones* employed a form of ⲙⲟⲟϣⲉ with a preposition, perhaps ⲙⲛ, which is rendered rather literally by the Arabic translator.
113 "Over him" or "for him." Barrett-Lennard, "Canons of Hippolytus", 154 n. 56, suggests that this reflects the ἐπ' αὐτόν of Jas 5:14.
114 Cf. Acts 5:15.
115 Literally "he is not to make the sick sleep in the dormitory"; Coquin suggests a confusion deriving from the Coptic, an optative being taken as causative. As argued in the introduction, this is taken as a hospice for the support of the poor rather than a hospital as such.

## القانون الخامس والعشرون

### لاجل اقامة وكيل المرضى من قبل الاسقف ولاجل اوقات الصلاة

الوكيل الذي يهتم بالمرضى فليعلهم الاسقف. حتى الاناء الفخار لاجل حاجة المرضى يدفعه الاسقف للوكيل.

ليكن كل واحد في رتبة النصارى يصلي حين قيامهم من النوم بكرة ويغسلوا ايديهم اذا ارادوا ان يصلوا ومن قبل ان يصنعوا شيئا. يصلوا ايضا في ثالث ساعة لانه الوقت الذي صلب فيه المخلص يسوع بارادته لخلاصنا حتى عتقنا. وايضا في الساعة السادسة يصلوا لانه الوقت الذي اضطربت فيه كل البرية لاجل الفعل السوء الذي فعله اليهود به. وفي الساعة التاسعة ايضا يصلوا لان المسيح صلى واسلم روحه في يدي ابيه في ذلك الوقت. وايضا في الوقت الذي تغيب فيه الشمس يصلوا لانه تمام اليوم. وايضا في اللخنيكن عشية فليصلوا لان داود يقول بالليل انطق. وايضا في نصف الليل ليصلوا فان داود ايضا فعل هذا وبولس وسيلاس خادما المسيح كانا يصليان في نصف الليل ويسبحان الله.

The twenty-fifth canon:
concerning the institution[116] of a steward for the sick by the bishop, and concerning the times of prayer

The steward is the one who takes care of the sick, so that the bishop can support them. The bishop even gives the clay pot, which the sick need, to the steward.

Every Christian, of any rank, is to pray on waking from sleep in the morning; they are to wash their hands when they wish to pray, and before they do anything. They are to pray again at the third hour, for it is the time when Jesus was willingly crucified, for our salvation and to set us free. And they pray again at the sixth hour since this is the time when the whole of creation was troubled on account of the wicked deed which the Jews did to him. At the ninth hour they shall pray because Christ prayed, and surrendered his spirit into the hands of his Father at that time. And they also pray as the sun goes down, because it is the end of the day.[117] And also in the evening, at the lamps (λυχνικόν), they pray since David said "I speak of you in the night."[118] They pray in the middle of the night, for David did this,[119] and Paul and Silas, servants of Christ; they were praying in the middle of the night and praising God.[120]

---

116  Although this word is not well attested, it is needed to make sense of the title.
117  Coquin notes that this is an addition to the *horarium* of *Traditio apostolica*, though Bradshaw suggests that the redactor may be confused by *Trad. ap.* 41.9 which makes the ninth hour the end of a day, and thus thought it applied to a further hour of prayer. It may be noted that these provisions are very close to those of *Testamentum Domini* 2.24, closer far than to *Traditio apostolica*, in that all the justifications centre on the passion. As such the addition, or confusion, may be the prayer at lamplighting, which seems to duplicate that at evening, and may have been derived from *Trad. ap.* 25, whereas that at the evening hour represents *Trad. ap.* 41.10, enjoining prayer at lying down to sleep.
118  Ps 77:6 (76:7).
119  Ps 119:62 (118:62), cited by Basil in *Reg. Fus.* 37 when discussing prayer at midnight.
120  Acts 16:25. The same justification is likewise given by Basil in *Reg. Fus.* 37.

## القانون السادس والعشرون

### لاجل استماع الكلام في الكنيسة والصلاة فيها

اذا كان في بيعة مفاوضة لاجل كلام الله فليسرع كل احد ويجتمع اليه وليعلموا ان هذا مصطفى لهم ان يسمعوا كلام الله اكثر من كل افتخار هذا العالم. وليعدوا انها خسارة عظيمة لهم اذا عاقتهم ضرورة ان يسمعوا كلام الله. بل يتفرغوا للكنيسة دفعات كثيرة ويقووا يخرجوا الحقد الذي للعدو ولا سيما اذا كان واحد يعرف يقرأ فانه يربح بالاكثر اذا سمع ما لم يكن يعرفه. لان الرب في الموضع الذي تذكر فيه الربوبية يحل الروح في المجتمعين وينعم على الكل والذين هم ذوو قلبين فيهم تطمأن عليهم لانك سمعت بعضهم بالروح. والذين يحركهم العقل في البيت فانهم لا يغفلوا عما سمعوه في الكنيسة. فلاجل هذا يجعل كل أحد همته ان يمضي الى الكنيسة في كل الايام التي تكون فيها الصلوات.

### القانون السابع والعشرون

لاجل من لا يمضي الى الكنيسة كل يوم يقرأ الكتب واي وقت صليت فاغسل يديك والحث على الصلاة نصف الليل وفي وقت يصيح الديك

## The twenty-sixth canon:
### concerning hearing the word in church, and the prayers therein

If there is a gathering in a church for the word of God let everyone hurry to meet there. They should know that to hear the word of God is better for them than all the glory of this world. They should count it great disadvantage to themselves if, out of necessity, they are prevented from hearing the words of God. Rather they should devote themselves to the church frequently, and be empowered to deflect the hatred of the enemy, especially if there is somebody who can read, for it is more advantageous to hear what one does not know. For the Lord, in the place where his majesty is recalled,[121] causes his Spirit to dwell in those who are assembled and endows all with his grace. And reassure those who have two hearts within them,[122] since you have heard some of them in the Spirit.[123] The minds of those who are disturbed at home do not forget what was heard in church; on this account it is important that everyone should go to church on all days when there are prayers.

## The twenty-seventh canon:
### concerning anyone who does not go daily to church, who should read Scripture; and that whenever you pray you should wash your hands; and concerning the exhortation to prayer in the middle of the night and at the time when the cock crows

---

121  Cf. *Did.* 4.1 and par.: ὅθεν γὰρ ἡ κυριότης λαλεῖται, ἐκεῖ κύριός ἐστιν.
122  Or, "You are reassured concerning those who have two hearts..." This is reminiscent of the warnings within the two-ways tradition of those who are "double-minded" such as *Apostolic church order* 13.2 (see below).
123  Coquin suggests that this obscure phrase may be illuminated from the two-ways tradition, in particular *Apostolic church order* 13.2: "In your prayer you shall not be divided in your mind, whether it will be or not". We may also note the parallel in *Barn.* 19.5a: "You shall not be divided in your mind, whether it will be or not."

وكل يوم لا يصلون في الكنيسة فتأخد كتابا وتقرأ فيه ولتنتظر الشمس الكتاب على رجليك كل الغدوات. والنصراني يغسل يديه في كل وقت يصلي والذين هم مرتبطون بالزيجة ولو انه حتى يقوم من عند زوجته فليصلي لان الزيجة غير نجسة ولا يحتاج الى حميم بماء من بعد الولادة الثانية ما خلا غسل اليدين لا غير لان روح القدس تشم جسد المؤمن وتطهره جميعه.

ليهتم كل أحد ان يصلي في تحفظ عظيم في نصف الليل لان آباؤنا قالوا ان في تلك الساعة تتفرغ كل البرية لخدمة مجد الله كل صفوف الملائكة وانفس الابرار يباركون الله لان الرب يشهد بهذا ويقول ان في نصف الليل كان صوت ان هو ذا الختن جاء اخرجوا للقائه. وفي وقت يصقع الديك ايضا هو وقت يكون الصلوات في الكنائس لان الرب هو القائل تحفظوا فانكم لا تدرون اي وقت يأتي الرب بالليل او نصف الليل او وقت يصيح الديك او الصبح. أي يجب علينا ان نذكر الله في كل الساعة. واذا كان الانسان راقدا على فراشه يجب عليه ان يصلي بقلبه لله.

نصنع هذا ونحن نعلم بعضنا بعضا مع المتعظين لخدمة الاله. ولا يتمكنون الشياطين يحزنونا اذا كنا نذكر المسيح في كل الساعة.

Those who do not go to the church should pick up the Scripture every day and read it; every morning the sun should see the Scripture on your knees.[124] Christians should wash their hands at every occasion of prayer; someone who is bound in marriage, even if he gets up from beside his wife, should pray nonetheless, as marriage is not unclean and he has no need of a bath in water after his second birth, except only the washing of hands, because the Holy Spirit scents[125] and cleanses the body of a believer entirely.

It should be everyone's concern to pray with great care in the middle of the night, since our fathers have said that at that hour the entire creation devotes itself to the service of the glory of God, all the ranks of angels and all the souls of the righteous bless God. Since the Lord witnesses to this in saying: "In the middle of the night there was a cry: 'The bridegroom has come; go out and meet him.'"[126] And at the time the cock crows, again that is a time when prayers take place in churches. For the Lord said: "Be watchful. For you do not know at what time the Lord will come, in the night,[127] or in the middle of the night, or the time when the cock crows, or in the morning."[128] It is thus incumbent on us to remember God at every hour. And if a person is lying on his bed he should pray to God[129] in his heart.

Let us do that, and let us instruct each other, with the catechumens, in the service of God. And the demons will not be able to grieve[130] us if we are mindful of Christ at every hour.

---

124 This phrase is absent in R.
125 Here reading *tašmimu*, the reading of m as printed by Coquin. d reads *taršumu*, which would mean "marks". R reads *tasmimu*, which would mean "to name", but is also a very slight corruption of the reading of m, the difference lying solely in diacritical marks. "Marks" is indeed the translation given by Coquin and Bebawi (in Bradshaw), whereas Haneberg has "odoratur" and Riedel "durchhaucht" (as here.) Although "marks" may well be the correct reading, "scents" is coherent; Wisdom is described in Scripture as having a fragrance (Sir 24:15; 39:13–14), and *Odes Sol.* 11.15 refers to the believer being scented, though given the reference to cleansing in this passage perhaps the most relevant parallel is *Const. ap.* 7.44, where the prayer at the post-baptismal anointing refers to the "sweet odour of the knowledge of the Gospel" and asks that the "sweet odour of your Christ" might continue on the newly baptized.
126 Matt 25:6.
127 So the text, though Coquin suggests that the text should read "evening", proposing that the Coptic ⲡⲟⲩϩⲉ has been mistranslated.
128 Mark 13:35.
129 R reads "should get up and pray to God."
130 So the text, *yaḥzubūnā*. However, serious consideration should be given to Coquin's suggested emendation to *yujrribūnā*, which would mean "test" or "tempt".

## القانون الثامن والعشرون

لا يذق أحد من المؤمنين شيئا الا بعد ان يتناول السرائر لا سيما في ايام الصوم

لا يذق أحد من المؤمنين شيئا الا بعد ان يتناول من السرائر ولا سيما في ايام الصوم.

وليتحفظ الاكليرسات لا يدعوا احدا ان يتناول من السرائر الا المؤمنين وحدهم.

## القانون التاسع والعشرون

لاجل حراسة المذبح لئلا يقع شيء في الكأس وان لا يسقط شيء من الكهنة ولا من المؤمنين لئلا يتسلط عليه روح خبيث ولا يتكلم أحد في الستارة الا صلاة واذا فرغوا مما يدفعون للشعب يكن كل من يدخل الى الموضع يقرأ المزامير عوضا من الجلاجل ولاجل رشم الصليب وتراب الهيكل يلقى في التيار

The twenty-eighth canon:
that none of the faithful should taste of anything until after he has eaten of the mysteries, especially not on the days of fasting

None of the faithful should taste of anything until after he has eaten of the mysteries, and especially not on days of fasting.[131]

The clergy (κλῆρος) should be careful not to permit anyone to eat of the mysteries apart from the faithful alone.

The twenty-ninth canon:
concerning vigilance at the altar,[132] that nothing should fall in the cup, and that nothing should fall on account of the priests or on account of the faithful, lest a wicked spirit should have power over it; and nobody should speak within the veil except for prayer; and when they finish communicating the congregation; when all they who enter the (holy) place they read psalms[133] instead of the bells; and concerning marking with the cross; and the dust of the temple is to be thrown into the stream[134]

---

131 Bradshaw is confused here because, according to Socrates *Hist. Eccl.* 5.22, there was no celebration of the Eucharist on fasting days in Alexandria. However, these days are explicitly stated to be days for eucharistic celebration in Cappadocia by *Test. Dom.* 1.22, supported by Basil *Ep.* 93, to Caesaria, who states that these are the days on which he communicates. The confusion is thus caused by the assumption of an Egyptian provenance.
132 m reads: "vigilance over the offerings placed on the altar." Note also the contents table above.
133 So R. m reads "the psalms should be recited in every place."
134 To the second part of this canon (that without origin in *Traditio apostolica*) cf. *Can. Bas.* 96: "A cleric should only speak at the altar when he has to speak, for Aaron made bells for himself on his clothing out of fear of the angels, but we have to use psalms at the altar in place of Aaron's bells. The earth which is swept from the altar should be thrown into the water of a flowing stream. Nobody should speak in choir, or around the altar." (Translated from the German of Riedel, *Kirchenrechtsquellen*, 272.)

وليقف الاكليرس متفرغا للمذبح اذا كان مستعدا يقف يحرسه لئلا يصعده دبيب او يقع شيء في الكأس فيكون وزر موت على القساء فلاجل هذا يكن واحد واقفا يحرس الموضع المقدس والذي يدفع السرائر والذين يتناولون يتحرزوا بثبات عظيم لئلا يسقط شيء على الارض يتسلط عليه روح خبيث.

ولا يتكلموا جملة من داخل الستارة الا صلاة لا غير وحوائج الخدمة ولا يفعلوا شيئًا في ذلك الموضع. ومن بعد ما يفرغون مما يدفعون للشعب يدخلوا ليرتلوا في كل ساعة يدخلون لاجل سلاطين الموضع المقدس. وتكن المزامير لهم عوضا من الجلاجل التي كانت في ثوب هرون. ولا يجلس في ذلك الموضع كل أحد الا صلاة لا غير وجثو الركب والسجود قدام المذبح.

والتراب الذي يكنس من الموضع المقدس يرموا في ماء بحر له تيار ولا يتوانوا لئلا يداسوا من الناس.

وتنقى كل وقت وترشم جبهتك مثال الصليب ظفرا بابليس وفخرا لامانتك صنع هذا موسى بدم الخروف هذا الذي لطخ به الاسكفات وعضادتي الابواب وشفى من كان ساكنا فيهم. فكيف بالاكثر لا يطهر ويحفظ بالاكثر دم المسيح للذين يؤمنون به

The clergy (κλῆρος) are to stand entirely occupied[135] with the altar when it has been prepared; they stand watchful lest any crawling thing[136] climb, or anything fall, into the cup, which would be a mortal error for the presbyters. For this reason those who stand in the holy place are to be watchful, and those who administer the mysteries and those who communicate should take great care that nothing fall to the ground, so that no malicious spirit should have power over it.

And they are not to speak a word within the veil,[137] except for prayer alone, and whatever is necessary for service. They are not to do[138] a thing in that place. And when they have finished communicating the congregation they enter; they intone every time they enter on account of the powers of the holy place. The psalms serve for them as the bells which were on Aaron's robe.[139] Nobody should sit down in that place; only prayer, kneeling, and prostrating before the altar.

And the dust which is swept from the holy place is thrown into water running in a stream; [140] there is to be no delay, lest[141] it be trodden on by people.

And be pure at all times, mark your forehead with the cross, the victory over the devil and the sign of your faith. Moses did this with the blood of the lamb, with which he daubed the lintel and the two door-posts, so healing anyone who lived there.[142] How should the blood of Christ not purify the better, and preserve the better, those who put their faith in it,

---

135 Coquin notes that the Arabic word *faraġa*, like the Coptic ⲥⲣϥⲉ, can mean to be unoccupied or occupied with nothing else than... thus "entirely occupied."
136 Coquin, followed by Bebawi (in Bradshaw), translates as "insect". However, the word *dabīb* means something that crawls, rather than flies, though this may include ants; however a lizard may equally be meant. Haneberg has *dhabib*, which he takes to mean "fly"; the form is not in the lexica, though "fly" (*dhubāba*) exists, though from a root meaning "to repel". We may suggest the influence of *Const. ap.* 8.12, which directs that deacons should stand with fans to ward off "flying animals." Emendation of *dabīb* to *dhubāba* might be considered, though the noun must remain singular, as otherwise the verb would also require emendation.
137 For the veiling of the altar see also *Test. Dom.* 1.19, 1.23.
138 Some MSS have "remove anything"; the Arabic words, *qal'a* (speak) and *f'ala* (act) are very similar in appearance.
139 Exod 28:35.
140 ⲟⲩⲉⲓⲟⲙ ⲉϥⲛ̄ⲧϥ̄ ⲟⲩⲙⲁⲛ̄ϩⲁⲁⲧⲉ. See the note on *baḥr* at n. 84 *supra*.
141 "Lest" is supplied following a conjecture of Coquin.
142 Exod 12:7.

ويبدوا مثل الخلاص الذي يكون لكل المسكونة الذي هو مؤسى بدم الخروف الكامل المسيح؟

كل السرائر لاجل الحياة والقيامة والذبيحة النصارى والنصارى وحدهم الذين يسمعون هذا لانهم نالوا الخاتم الذي للمعمودية لانهم الشركاء.

### القانون الثلاثون

### لاجل المتعظين

الموعوظون يسمعوا الكلام لاجل الامانة والتعليم فقط. هذا هو التزكية التي قال يوحنا ان ليس أحد يعرفها الا الذي يقبلها.

يوم الاحد في وقت القداس ان قدر الاسقف فليقرب كل الشعب من يده.

وان كان قسيس مريضا فيمضي له الشماس بالسرائر والقسيس يأخذ له وحده.

### القانون الحادي والثلاثون

لاجل الاسقف والقسيس اذا آمرا الشماس ان يقرب الشعب يقرب ويقرب الشماس الشعب اذا اذن له الاسقف او القسيس.

and make the sign of salvation which is for the whole world,[143] which is healed by the blood of Christ, the perfect lamb?

Christians alone are to hear all the mysteries concerning life, the resurrection and the sacrifice, because theirs is the seal of baptism, in which they have participated.

### The thirtieth canon: concerning the catechumens

The catechumens hear the word concerning the faith and instruction only. This is the decision[144] of which John spoke: "Nobody knows of it except the one who accepts it."[145]

On the first day, at the time of the liturgy, the bishop, if he is able, should communicate the entire congregation with his hand.

If a presbyter is sick, the deacon brings the mysteries to him, and the presbyter takes them himself.[146]

### The thirty-first canon: concerning the bishop and the presbyter, when they instruct the deacon to communicate the people, and he communicates

The deacon communicates the people when the bishop or the presbyter authorizes him.

---

143 Riedel suggests that *almaskuwnati* here renders τῆς οἰκουμένης.
144 It would perhaps be better to correct this to "stone." Coquin suggests that ψῆφος, the word we would expect here on the basis of sense and the other versions of *Traditio apostolica*, has been misunderstood and taken in its secondary sense.
145 Rev 2:17.
146 This provision is a rewriting of a provision in *Trad. ap.* 22 regarding the carrying of the *fermentum* between the churches of Rome. Since the provision is incomprehensible outside of this context, the redactor of *Canones Hippolyti* has taken this to refer to the controverted practice of deacons administering Communion to presbyters, a practice outlawed by the eighteenth canon of Nicaea. Since the practice appeared to be permitted in *Traditio apostolica* (though this was not the original intent) the material has been adjusted to refer to a presbyter in sickness.

## القانون الثاني والثلاثون

لاجل العذارى والارامل يصمن ويصلين في الكنيسة والاكليريكسات يصوموا باختيارهم والاسقف لا يربط بصوم الا مع الاكليرس ولاجل وليمة او عشاء يصلح للفقراء

العذارى والارامل يصمن دفعات كثيرة ويصلين في الكنيسة والاكليريكسات يصوموا باختيارهم وسلطانهم والاسقف فلا يربط بصوم الا ان يكون الاكليرس يصوم معه.

واذا اراد واحد ان يصنع قربانا اذا لم يكن قسيس حاضرا في الكنيسة فيكن الشماس عوضا منه في كل شيء ما خلا حمل الذبيحة العظيمة وحدها والصلاة.

واذا دفع قربان ليدفع الصدقة الى الفقراء يعطوا من قبل ان تغرب الشمس لفقراء الشعب. فادا فضل شيء ضرورة فيدفعوا في الغد فادا فضل منهم شيء اليوم الثالث. فلا يحسب شيء منهم لمن هو في بيته بل الرحمة كلها تحسب لصاحبها وحده الذي يدفع لا ينل لان خبز الفقير بات في بيته بتوانيه.

The thirty-second canon:
concerning virgins and widows, fasting and praying in the church;[147] and that the clergy (κληρικός) fast at their discretion, and the bishop is not bound to fast except with the clergy (κλῆρος); concerning a dinner or a feast suitable for the poor

Virgins and widows fast on many occasions, and pray in the church. The clergy (κληρικός) fast at their discretion and according to their ability, and the bishop is not bound to fast, unless the clergy (κλῆρος) are fasting with him.[148]

If anyone wishes to make an offering and no presbyter is present in the church then the deacon shall take his place in everything except the lifting[149] of the great sacrifice and the prayer.

If an offering is given to be distributed as charity to the poor it should be distributed before the sun sets to the poor of the people. If there is surplus beyond requirement it should be distributed the next day, and if anything is left, on the third day. Nothing is accredited to him on account of the fact that it was in his house; the whole of the mercy is for the originator of the gift, since the bread of the poor remained in his house through his delay.[150]

---

147 "In the church": so the text, though Coquin translates as "pour" as the corresponding section of *Traditio apostolica* has ὑπέρ. However, in keeping with *Testamentum Domini* we may see this as representing the practice of female ascetics.
148 Achelis suggests that κλῆρος here is an error, and that it should be "the people" (so *Traditio apostolica*.) Whereas this is plausible, we should also note the close relationship in this community between bishop and presbyters as forming an ascetic community. Thus it is also possible that this constitutes a deliberate alteration on the part of the redactor.
149 A rather literal rendering is given here, though Coquin suggests that this represents the Coptic ⲧⲁⲗⲟ ⲉϩⲣⲁⲓ, and represents an over-literal rendering of ἀναφορά.
150 Coquin struggles to understand this, though the direction of thought in the Aksumite Ethiopic of *Traditio apostolica* (which was not available to Coquin), alongside the version of this in *Testamentum Domini* 2.11, makes the original on which it is based reasonably clear, and as a result allows us to understand the canonist's expansion. The point in *Traditio apostolica* is that if goods are delayed in transit, the person responsible should supplement the gift, on the grounds that *he* had held back bread meant for the poor. Here it seems that the idea has arisen that there is some merit in having these gifts in one's possession, which the canonist is at pains to deny; the spiritual benefit accrues solely to the donor. Coquin suggests that the agent is claiming the spiritual benefit due to the donor; I think it more possible that there was some confusion between these gifts and the eucharistic species, and that the gifts, seen as eucharistic, are thought to have brought a blessing by being present in a house.

اذا كان وليمة او عشاء صنعه واحد للفقراء وهو كيرياكن فيكن الاسقف حاضرا وقت يوقد سراج. ويقم الشماس ليوقده فيصلي الاسقف عليهم وعلى الذي دعاهم. ويجب للفقراء الاوخارسدية التي في اول القداس ويصرفوهم لينفردوا من قبل ان يكون الظلام ويصنعوا مزامير من قبل مضيهم.

If there is a feast or a dinner provided by somebody for the poor, it is the Lord's (κυριακόν).¹⁵¹ The bishop should be present when a lamp is lit. The deacon gets up to light it and the bishop prays over them and over those who invited them. It is right that he make the thanksgiving (εὐχαριστία) at the beginning of the liturgy¹⁵² so that they can be dismissed before it is dark, and recite psalms before their departure.

151 It is not clear what is meant here. Reference back to *Traditio apostolica* does not assist, as although this paragraph is clearly derived from *Trad. ap.* 25 the beginning of the paragraph appears to be redactional. Riedel, followed by Bradshaw, suggests that the word δεῖπνον is understood, though we may note that this term does not necessarily imply a eucharistic celebration. This understanding may receive some support from the usage in *Can. Hipp.* 34 below, though in this instance the Eucharist may be meant, and the entire phrase is directly derived from *Trad. ap.* 27. Haneberg (122) suggests that the text should be read as κυριακήν (thus the feast takes place on a Sunday), though not only does this require emendation of the text, but it does not fit with the usage ("the first day") in the next canon. The suggestion of Jourdan, "'Agape' or 'Lord's supper'", 41, that it simply means "something of the Lord" does not answer the question. A possibility is that it should be read as some corrupted form of ἐν τῷ κυριακῷ, and thus intend a meal in the church. This is possible; if the Greek original read something like ἐν τῷ κυριακῷ, then the textual corruption in a Coptic version from "and it is in the..." to "and it is" is relatively simple. Jourdan, "'Agape' or 'Lord's supper'", 40, states that this does not fit the context well, but it seems that a supper for the poor held in a church would make perfect sense, since the 28th canon of the Council of Laodicea specifically legislates against holding *agapae* ἐν τοῖς κυριακοῖς.

152 Such is the rendition of Coquin. Arendzen, "The XXXII Canon of Hippolytus," 284, however, suggests that the form of the verb (form 1, the base form), used with a following preposition (as it is here) is odd, and that the verb should be read as a form 4 (usually causative, like the Hebrew *piel*), thus meaning: "He should have the poor say the thanksgiving at the beginning..." In either event the meaning of the statement is obscure. The word translated "liturgy" is that generally employed in the *Canones* for the eucharistic liturgy (*quddās*). Thus the phrase could mean either that he is to conduct the eucharistic liturgy at the beginning of the meal (so, apparently, Riedel, Lietzmann, *Messe und Herrenmahl*, 199-200) or that he is to say certain words as a grace (so Jourdan, "'Agape or 'Lord's supper'", 37-38), the same as those found at the beginning of the eucharistic liturgy (Cirlot, *The early Eucharist*, 183, Bradshaw.) This latter suggestion finds support, as Bradshaw notes, from *Traditio apostolica*, in which there is a dialogue with similarity to the opening eucharistic dialogue. Although Arendzen's suggestion is not adopted here, we may note that he likewise takes *āwkhristiya* to refer to a grace, and suggests that the poor might be enjoined to say it as the words would be familiar from the liturgy.

القانون الثالث والثلاثون

لاجل انالمسيس يصنعونه عن الذين ماتوا ولا يكن ذلك في يوم الاحد

وان كانت انالمسيس يصنعونها عنهم الذين ماتوا فينالوا اولا من السرائر من قبل ان يجلسوا. ليس يوم الاحد. ومن بعد القربان يدفع لهم خبز اكسركسمس من قبل ان يجلسوا.

ولا يجلس معهم واحد من المتعظين في الولائم الكيرياكن.

ويأكلوا ويشربوا بكفاف ولا بسكر بل بالسكينة مجدا لله.

القانون الرابع والثلاثون

لا يتكلم احد كثيرا ولا يصيح ولاجل دخول القديسين الى منازل المؤمنين

لا يتكلم أحد كثيرا ولا يصيح ولا يهزأوا بكم ولئلا تكونوا عثرة للناس ويشتم من دعاكم لاجل انكم على غير الطقس. بل هو ايضا يدعوه ينال وكل بيته ويرى عفاف كل واحد منا وينل

The thirty-third canon:
concerning the ἀνάλημψις which is kept for those who have died, and that this should not be on the first day

If there is an ἀνάλημψις which is kept for those who have died,[153] they should receive first of the mysteries, before they sit down. This does not occur on the first day. After the offering, the bread of exorcism (ἐξορκισμός) is given them, before they sit down.

None of the catechumens should be seated with them at the suppers of the Lord (κυριακόν).

They should eat and drink with sufficiency, not to intoxication, in serenity, to the glory of God.

The thirty-fourth canon:
that nobody should talk overmuch or call out; and concerning the entry of the saints into the homes of the faithful

Nobody is to talk overmuch, nor call out, so that they cannot make fun of you, so that you are not a stumbling-block to the people, and the one who invited you is grieved because you are disorderly.[154] He, and all his household, should be allowed to participate,[155] and recognize the decency of all of us, and obtain

---

153 The text simply transliterates the Greek word as *ānālmsīs*. Haneberg emends to ἀνάμνησις, as indeed does Reicke, *Diakonie*, 101. Coquin, in retaining the term, believes this refers to the death of those who are remembered, pointing to the use at Luke 9:51 to indicate that the word might mean "departure", though comments that the context would indicate a liturgical event. He suggests that the word is employed in this manner in *Const. ap.* 6.30.2 (ἐξόδοις) and in *Didasc. ap.* 6.22.2, ܟܘܡܣܐ, thus reflecting this usage, but here it refers to the passing of the deceased, rather than to the funeral rites. Rather than referring to the death commemorated (which would be otiose, given that the funeral context is then made clear) is it possible that this is the term employed in the community for such an occasion? There is a possible parallel for this use of the word in a third-century inscription from Thrace (SIG 888.39–44), in which villagers are complaining to Gordian about the depredations of troops, and state that "they come to our village and force us to provide them lodgings and everything else for their provision (καὶ ἕτερα πλεῖστα εἰς ἀνάλημψιν αὐτῶν) without payment of any monies." In other words, the ἀνάλημψις is an entertainment or provision, specifically here an entertainment on the anniversary of a death or at a funeral.
154 Literally without τάξις.
155 Literally "to receive"; the translator is confused by the dual sense of Coptic ϫɪ.

رتبة عظيمة بالمثال الذي يراه علينا ويصلي ان يدخل القديسون تحت سقفه لان مخلصنا يقول انتم ملح الارض.

واذا قال الاسقف كلاما وهو جالس فانهم يربحوا به ويربح. وان كان ليس الاسقف حاضرا والقسيس حاضرا فليلتفتوا كلهم اليه لانه ارفع منهم بالله ويكرموه الكرامة التي يكرم بها الاسقف ولا يجسروا يقاوموه. ويعطهم خبز اكسركسمس من قبل ان يجلسوا لكي ينجي الله وليمتهم من القلق الذي للعدو ويقوموا وهم صحاح بسلام.

### القانون الخامس والثلاثون

لاجل شماس حاضر في وليمة وليس قسيس حاضرا يكن عوضا منه في الصلاة وكسر الخبز للبركة وليس للجسد واصراف الارامل قبل العشاء

شماس في وليمة وليس قسيس حاضرا يصر عوضا من القسيس في الصلاة على الخبز يكسره ويدفعه للمدعيين. فاما العلماني فلم يدفع له ان يرشم الخبز بل يكسره لا غير واذا لم يكن هناك اكليركس.

فليأكل كل واحد مما يأتي كل بشكر باسم الله لكي يروا الامم سيرتكم فيحسدوكم.

a mighty rank[156] through the example which he sees us set. He will desire the saints to come under his roof, since, as our Saviour says, "You are the salt of the earth."[157]

If the bishop says a word while they are seated they are to profit from it, and he will profit. If no bishop is present and a presbyter is present they should all turn to him because he is more exalted in God than they; they honour him with the honour with which they honour the bishop and not dare to resist him. Before they sit down he is to give them the bread of exorcism (ἐξορκισμός) so that God can set their feast free of any troubles from the enemy, and be righteous, in peace, when they get up.

The thirty-fifth canon:
concerning a deacon present at a supper, and no presbyter is present, he is to take his place for the prayer and for the breaking of bread, for the blessing, but not for the body; and the dismissal of widows before the evening

A deacon present at supper, where there is no presbyter, takes his place for the prayer over the bread. He breaks it and gives it to those who have been invited. A layman is not to make the sign[158] over the bread but only to break it, and[159] only if no cleric (κληρικός) is present.

Everyone is to eat of what is brought[160] with all thanksgiving in the name of God, so that the nations may see your conduct,[161] and be envious of you.[162]

---

156 *Rutba* here, as Coquin suggests, certainly represents κλῆρος; thus "share" might be a better translation. Bebawi (in Bradshaw) gives "blessing."
157 Matt 5:13.
158 Literally, "to mark".
159 Coquin deletes this "and".
160 So R. m reads "eat of what he eats".
161 Reading *sayratakum*, the reading of m. Coquin reads *saryratakum* ("their desires", or "their thoughts") with R. The thinking here is that *saryra* refers to inward disposition, which cannot be seen.
162 As in canon 19 above, Arabic *ḥasada* (be envious) here represents ⲕⲱϩ, which in turn represents ζηλοῦν, which might mean either "envy" or "imitate". The second meaning is probably that originally intended.

واذا اراد واحد ان يطعم ارامل فيطعمهن ويصرفهن من قبل ان تغرب الشمس. وان كن كثيرا لئلا يتبلبلن وانهن لا يلحقن ينصرفن من قبل العشاء فليدفع لكل واحدة منهن كفافها ما تأكله وتشربه ويمضين من قبل ان يمسي الليل.

## القانون السادس والثلاثون

لاجل ابكار ثمار الارض واول اندرهم ومعاصرهم والزيت والعسل واللبن والصوف وغير ذلك مما يمضي به الى الاسقف ليبارك عليه

وابكار اثمار الارض من كان له فليمضي به الى الكنيسة واوائل اندرهم واوائل معاصرهم والزيت والعسل واللبن والصوف واوائل اجرة عمل ايديهم هؤلاء كلهم يمضوا بهم نحو الاسقف واوائل اشجارهم. والكاهن الذي يأخذهم يشكر الله عليهم اولا خارجا عن الستارة والذي احضرهم قائمًا.

ويقول الكاهن. نشكرك يا رب الله ضابط الكل لانك جعلتنا مستحقين ان ننظر الى هذه الثمار التي اخرجتها الارض في هذه السنة بارك يا رب اكليل السنة التي لصلاحك ويكونوا شبعا لفقراء شعبك وعبدك فلان هذا الذي اتى بهولاء مما لك لابه خائف منك باركه من سمائك المقدسة وكل بيته. وتفيض عليه رحمتك المقدسة ليعرف ارادتك في كل شيء وتجعله يرث ما في السموات. بربنا يسوع المسيح ابنك الحبيب وروح القدس الى ابد الابدين. آمين.

If anyone wishes to feed widows, he should feed them and dismiss them before the sun sets. And if they are numerous, so that they should not become restive and unable to leave before evening, he should give them enough to eat and drink, and they should depart before the onset of the night.[163]

The thirty-sixth canon:
concerning the first-fruits of the earth, and the first of their threshing-floors and presses, and the oil, the milk, the honey, the wool, and the other things that should be taken to the bishop for his blessing on them

Whoever has first-fruits of the land should bring them to the church, the first of their threshing-floors, the first of their presses, the oil, the honey, the milk, and the wool, and the first of what they have earned by the labour of their hands, all of these are brought to the bishop, as well as the first from their trees. And the priest who takes them gives thanks to God for them first, outside the veil, while the one who has brought them stands.[164]

And the priest says: "We give you thanks Lord, all powerful God, since you have made us worthy to look upon these fruits which the earth has brought forth this year. Bless, Lord, the crown of the year of your bounty:[165] may they provide satisfaction for the poor of your people. And bless from your holy heaven your servant N, who out of fear of you has brought these things, which are yours, and all his house.[166] Pour out your holy mercy on him, that he may know your will in all things, and make him an inheritor of what is in the heavens. Through our Lord Jesus Christ, your beloved Son, and the Holy Spirit, to the ages of the ages. Amen."

---

163 This is close to *Traditio apostolica*, but note also *Didasc. ap.* 2.28.1: "Those who wish to give an agape (ܐܓܦܐ), and to invite the widows, should send more frequently for her whom he knows to be in distress. And if anyone gives gifts to widows he should especially send to her whom he knows to be in need."
164 Possibly, as Coquin suggests, the text originally read something along the lines of "...gives thanks to God for them first, while the one who brought them stands outside the veil."
165 Ps 65:11 (64: 12) cited in the *Liturgy of St Mark* (Jasper & Cuming, *Prayers of the Eucharist*, 61) in a similar manner: "Bless, Lord, the crown of the year of your goodness, for the poor of your people..."
166 So d. R has "his children", and m "his house and his children."

وكل بقولات وكل فواكه الاشجار وكل ثمار المقاثئ يبارك عليهم ومن ياتي بهم ببركة.

### القانون السابع والثلاثون

لاجل كل دفعة ينال الاسقف السرائر تجتمع الشمامسة والقساء وهم لابسون ثيابا بيضا ابهى من كل الشعب وكذلك الاغنستسيون

وكل دفعة ينال الاسقف من السرائر تجتمع الشمامسة والقساء اليه وهم الابسون ثيابا بيضا ابهى من كل الشعب ومضيئون بالاكثر بافعالهم الحسنة اكثر من الثياب.

والاغنستسيون ايضا يكونوا بهيين مثل هولاء ويقفوا في موضع القراءة ويبدلوا بعضهم بعضا الى ان تجتمع جميع الشعب وبعد ذلك يصلي الاسقف ويكمل القداس.

All vegetables, all fruits of trees, and all produce of cucumber beds is to be blessed, along with those who bring them, with a blessing.

The thirty-seventh canon:
concerning each occasion on which the bishop offers[167] the mysteries, the deacons and the presbyters are to meet dressed in white garments more glorious than the people; and also the readers (ἀναγνώστης)

Every time that the bishop offers[168] the mysteries the deacons and the presbyters gather with him whilst dressed in white garments more glorious than all the people, and more luminous yet in their noble deeds than in their clothing.

The readers (ἀναγνώστης) also are as glorious as these, and they stand at the place of reading and take turns until the people is assembled; and after this the bishop prays and completes the liturgy.

---

167 Literally "takes"; again a mistranslation of Coptic ϫⲓ.
168 As in the title, literally "takes", mistranslating Coptic ϫⲓ.

## القانون الثامن والثلاثون

لاجل الليلة التي قام فيها ربنا لا ينم احد في تلك الليلة ويستحم بالماء ولاجل من يخطأ بعد المعمودية وشرح ذلك والنهي عما لا يجب وفعل ما يجب

فاما ليلة قيامة ربنا فليكن احتراز عظيم حتى انه لا ينام احد جملة الى بكرة. ثم يغسلوا اجسادهم بماء من قبل ان يحلوا الفصح وليكن كل الشعب ينور. لان في تلك الساعة جعل المخلص كل البرية احرارا وعبد ما للسموات وما للارضين وكلما فيهم لانه قام من الاموات وصعد الى السموات وجلس عن يمين الله ويأتي في مجد ابيه وملائكته ويجازي كل واحد كاعماله الذين صنعوا الخير قيامة حياة والذين فعلوا السيئات قيامة دينونة كما هو مكتوب. فلاجل هذا يجب علينا ان نكون متيقظين كل حين ولا نعطي عيننا نوما ولا جفننا نعاسا الى ان نجد موضعا للرب.

## The thirty-eighth canon:
concerning the night on which Our Lord rose; that nobody should sleep on that night, and they should bathe in water; concerning anyone who sins after baptism, and the explanation of that, and the prohibition of what should not be done, and the performance of what should be done

As regards the night of the resurrection of our Lord, great care should be taken that nobody sleeps at all until the morning. They are to wash their bodies with water before they accomplish the Pascha,[169] and all the people should be illuminated. For at that hour the Saviour made all the creation free, and subjugated the heavens and the earth and all that is in them,[170] when he was raised from the dead, and ascended to the heavens, and sat at the right hand of God. And he will come in the glory of his Father and his angels and will recompense everybody in accordance with their deeds,[171] those who acted well with the resurrection of life, and those who did evil with the resurrection of condemnation, as it is written.[172] For this reason it is right that we should be vigilant at all times, and that we should give no sleep to our eyes, or rest to our eyelids, until we have found a place for the Lord.[173]

---

169 Bradshaw asks, "Was this simply because they had presumably also abstained from the bath during the pre-paschal week of fasting or did it have some ritual significance?" We may point to ps-Clement *Hom.* 11.1, 11.28, as indicating the possibility of a ritual bath before worship as part of the regimen of purity known in this community, though this may be seen in contradiction to *Can. Hipp.* 27. In part such contradictions can be put down to the tension between the source text, *Traditio apostolica*, from which the provisions of *Can. Hipp.* 27 are taken, and the community for which the *Canones* were produced.
170 This is the reading of R. d has a reading with some distinctions though of the same meaning, whereas m reads: "the heavenly things and the earthly things rejoice" through what looks like a misreading of the verb.
171 Matt 16:27.
172 John 5:29. The text given is that of R, following Coquin. M and d conform the text to that of John through adding "to", though as Coquin points out the word *jazā* is doubly transitive.
173 Cf. Ps 132:4-5 (131:4-5).

لئلا يقول واحد انني تعمدت ونلت من جسد الرب ويطمأن ويقول اني نصراني ويصير هذا محبا للاغراض ولا يلتفت الى وصايا المسيح ويكون مثل واحد دخل الى حمام وهو ممتلئ وسخا ويخرج وكذلك يتدلك ولم يخرج وسخه عليه دفعة اخرى لانه لم يقبل اليه احتراق الروح كما يقول الطوباني الرسول انا نغلي بالروح. وكلمن ليس سريرته متيقظة فانها تكون محترقة الذي هو انها ليس هي حية في الخير بل هي ميتة في الاغراض. وصاروا كورا الذي هو هزؤ لابليس لانهم قالوا في افمامهم من الاول انا نرفضك يا ابليس والآن هم مسرعون اليه بافعالهم السيئة. وحقا انك لا تجد ابليس يفرح بمن عنده وهم منسوبون اليه مثل الذين هم عندنا بالجسد وهم معه بانفسهم هؤلاء الذين تكلم الرسول لاجلهم انهم معترفون انهم يعرفون الله ويجحدونه بافعالهم. ويقال لاجلهم في الامثال انه مثل كلب يرجع في قيئه وحده هكذا مثل الجاهل في شره اذا رجع الى خطاياه. الطوباني بطرس يقول لاجلهم انهم مثل خنزيرة استحمت ثم تقلبت في طينها. وليس هو وزر قليل ان يقول واحد امام الله اني لأفعل هواك كله ونصيبه يخدم ابليس ايضا في اغراض قبيحة. مثل جندي اذا قبل شكل الجندية ولا يهتم بآلة الجندية وكسوتها فانه يكون مفتضحا ولو انه يسمي نفسه وحده جنديا وليس له زي الجندية بل الشكل الذي هو يدعى به.

Thus[174] somebody who says "I have been baptized and received the Body of the Lord" and feels comfortable, and says "I am a Christian", yet is a lover[175] of selfish desires and is not conformed to the commandments of Christ, is like somebody who goes into a bath covered in dirt, and leaves without rubbing himself, since he did not receive the burning of the Spirit. As the blessed apostle says: "We are boiling over with the Spirit."[176] So anyone who is not minded towards vigilance is consumed, that is he is not living well but is dead in selfish desires. They are become balls,[177] that is the devil's plaything, for they initially said "we reject you O devil" with their mouths, and now they are rushing in his direction through their wicked deeds. Indeed, the devil does not rejoice over those who are his, and are of his race, as he does over those who are ours in the body but his in the spirit, of whom the apostle spoke: "They claim that they know God, but deny him in their deeds."[178] It is said in Proverbs concerning them that "like a dog returning to its own vomit is an ignorant person in his evil when he returns to his wrongdoing."[179] Blessed Peter says concerning them: "They are like a sow which bathes and then rolls in her mud."[180] It is no small matter if somebody should say before God "I will perform your wishes entirely" and participates in[181] the service of the devil anew in repulsive desires. Such is like a soldier who receives the mark of the army,[182] who has no interest in the equipment or the uniform of a soldier, and is found out, even if he calls himself a soldier, for he does not have a soldier's costume, but the mark by which he claims to be one.[183]

---

174 Literally "so that"; a misunderstanding of Coptic ϩⲱⲥⲧⲉ, which has the same meaning and function as Greek ὥστε.
175 Literally "becomes loving...". A Copticism.
176 Rom 12:11.
177 A possible translation (that of Coquin), as is "they are become an oven" (Haneberg and Riedel). Neither is fully convincing, but I have no reasonable emendation to offer.
178 Titus 1:16.
179 Prov 26:11.
180 2 Pet 2:22.
181 Literally "his share".
182 What exactly the mark of the army should be is not clear. The Arabic word, as discussed in n. 37 above, is šakl, meaning outward appearance, form, or shape. Coquin suggests that the Greek might originally have been σφραγίς; here that is probable, since the point of comparison is clearly intended to be baptism.
183 Vocalizing the verb as idda'ā. Alternatively it might be vocalized as du'iya and the phrase translated as "by which he is called one" (so Coquin).

هكذا واحد يقول عنه وحده انه نصراني وليس هو لابس الفعال فانه يسمي من الله ومن الناس شيطان لانه لم يبغض افعال الشياطين بل يثبت فيهم ولاجل هذا ينال اسمهم هاهنا ونصيبهم في الموضع الاخر. ويقول لهم المخلص في ذلك اليوم تباعدوا عني يا ملاعين الى النار الابدية المعدة لابليس وملائكته. لانهم كما احبوا افعاله على الارض وبقوا مختلطين معه في حياتهم هكذا يكونون في الجحيم اذا ماتوا في اغراضهم الطمثة.

In the same way somebody who claims to be a Christian, but does not clothe himself in the deeds is called "Satan" by God and by people[184] because he does not despise satanic acts, but flourishes in them. On this account they receive that name of theirs, and their lot in the other place. To them shall the Saviour say on that day: "Get away from me, you accursed, to the eternal fire prepared for the devil and his angels."[185] Because they loved his deeds on earth, and associated with him in their lives, so they shall find themselves in Gehenna if they die in their impure desires.

---

184 Cf. *Sent. Conc. Nic.* 1.11-12: "A man's inclination (προαίρεσις) is in his deeds. Thus some men are called angels (ἄγγελος) and some called demons (δαίμων)."
185 Matt 25:41.

لان النصراني يجب عليه ان يكون سائرا في وصايا المسيح متشبها بالله كاولاد احباء متشبها بالمسيح في كل شيء. لا يسب ولا يكن زانيا ولا يكن يهزأ ولا وقاعا ولا يعيب بالفوارغ ولا يكن دغلا ولا يشتته ما يهلك ولا يكن حرونا ولا محبا للربح ولا يحبس بانفه على احد ولا متذمرا ولا يدن اشياء غيره ولا يفرق ميراثه فيما ليس فيه خلاص ولا عمالا لما لا يجب ولا يكن قليل الرحمة ولا يشهد بالزور ولا يكن محبا لتكرمته ولا يكن منتهرا ولا سكيرا ولا يكن نهما ولا محبا للعالم ولا محبا للنساء بل يتزوج بامرأة واحدة ولا يكن يحسد ولا يكن يتوانى عن الكنائس ويربي اولاده بخوف الله ولا يهرب من التجارب. يكن يقرأ ويتأمل ما يسمعه ويكن يقنع

Because the Christian should be one who walks in the path of the commandments of Christ, conformed to God as beloved children, conformed to Christ in every regard, he does not speak evil,[186] and nor is he a fornicator,[187] nor scornful, nor a slanderer, nor a fault-finder,[188] he is not corrupt,[189] nor longs for what is perishable, he is not obstinate, nor a lover of gain,[190] nor haughty,[191] nor a grumbler,[192] nor pronouncing judgement in matters which are not his concern,[193] nor spending his inheritance where there is no salvation,[194] nor labouring at what is not proper, nor unmerciful,[195] nor bearing false witness.[196] Nor should he be someone who loves honour,[197] nor should he be quarrelsome,[198] nor a drunkard.[199] He is not greedy, nor a lover of the world,[200] nor a womanizer,[201] but he should be married to a single woman.[202] He is not envious. He is not slack with regard to the assemblies,[203] and he raises his children in the fear of God,[204] nor does he shrink from trials.[205] He is one who reads, and meditates on what he hears.[206]

---

186 *Sabba* has a wide range of meaning. My suggestion is that here it reflects καταλογέω (*Did.* 2.3 and par.)
187 Possibly πόρνος (*Did.* 2.2 and par.)
188 Literally, "not accusing somebody of vain matters." Possibly this has derived from μνησίκακος (*Did.* 2.3).
189 The meaning of this word is uncertain.
190 Coquin suggests αἰσχροκερδής (1 Tim 3:8; Titus 1:7; *Apostolic church order* 21.2.) We might also consider μηδὲ φιλάργυρος (*Did.* 3.5 and par.)
191 Literally "Do not turn up your nose at anyone". Since this Coptic idiom generally renders μυκτηρίζειν Coquin suggests that this is the underlying Greek. However, it may be a paraphrastic rendering of ὑψηλόφθαλμος (*Did.* 3.3 and par.) or οὐχ ὑψώσεις σεαυτόν (*Did.* 3.9 and par.)
192 μὴ γίνου γόγγυσος (*Did.* 3.6 and par.)
193 Literally "do not judge other matters", though other MSS have "do not judge strange matters, and "do not judge other people." In view of this final reading, is it possible that ὑποκριτής (*Did.* 2.6 and par.) lies behind this statement?
194 An allusion to Eph 5:18.
195 Literally "slight in mercy"; Cf. *Did.* 3.8.
196 *Did.* 2.3 and par.
197 Coquin suggests φιλότιμος.
198 *Did.* 3.2.
199 Titus 1:7; 1 Tim 3:3
200 Coquin reasonably suggests that this reflects φιλόκοσμος, a lover of finery; cf. n. 64 *supra*.
201 Literally "a lover of women".
202 1 Tim 3:2, Titus 1:6.
203 Literally "the churches".
204 Cf. *Did.* 4.9 and par.
205 Cf. *Did.* 3.10.
206 Cf. *Did.* 3.7 and par.

ولا يكن ظالما ولا تسرع يده للضرب بل يدفع ما عليه سريعا لئلا تجدف على اسم الله ولا يكن كسلانا ولا ينسى المحتاجين الذين يلتمسون منه ولا يفشي سره ولا يغير حدودا ولا يكن مرائيا بل محبا للغرباء ولا يهون بعبيده بل يعدهم مثل اولاده ولا يكن صعبا في تناوله واعطائه ولا يدع له ميزانين ولا مكيالين. ولا يتوانى عن القرابين والبكور ولا يعامل احدا من الاميين ولا يخالطهم ويكن عمالا خادما لله ولا يخرج عن اوامر انجيل الله هذا الذي بشر به في الخليقة كلها التي تحت السماء.

And he is somebody who is content.²⁰⁷ He is not oppressive, nor is his hand quick to administer a beating, but he quickly pays what he owes so that the name of God is not blasphemed.²⁰⁸ He is not idle, nor does he forget the needy who ask of him,²⁰⁹ nor divulge his secret, nor alter a boundary. He is not a usurer,²¹⁰ but loves the stranger;²¹¹ nor does he despise his slaves but treats them like his children. He is not ungracious in his giving and his receiving,²¹² he does not employ²¹³ two scales or measures,²¹⁴ nor does he neglect the offerings or the first-fruits,²¹⁵ nor has any commerce with any of the gentiles, nor mix with them.²¹⁶ He should be a worker in the service of God, not departing from the commands of the Gospel of God, that which has been proclaimed to the entire creation under the heavens.²¹⁷

207 Possibly meaning "is abstemious, temperate." This is the reading of R. d gives "is not anxious", whereas the phrase is absent from m.
208 Although the meaning of this sentence is coherent, given the other connections to the TWT material, and the difficult connection between the hand stretched out for beating, and the payment of debts, one cannot help wondering whether this is a garbled version of Did. 4.5: μὴ γίνου πρὸς μὲν τὸ λαβεῖν ἐκτείνων τὰς χεῖρας, πρὸς δὲ τὸ δοῦναι συσπῶν. Against this consideration is the catchword "quick."
209 Cf. Did. 4.8.
210 Murābyānu, the reading of md. One might prefer the reading of R, marāyi'ānu, "hypocrite".
211 φιλόξενος, thus possibly to be rendered as "hospitable."
212 Coquin notes an allusion to Sir 41:21, though we may also note, again, Did. 4.5 and par.
213 Literally "does not put down for himself"; a Copticism.
214 Deut 25:13; Prov 20:10, 23.
215 The giving of first-fruits in the context of righteous business dealings appears in Syntagma doctrinae and Fides patrum.
216 R reads "speak to them." A relatively minor difference between yakhalituhum and yakhatibuhum.
217 The allusion to Col 1:23 is clear, though there is also more than an echo of Did. 4.13 and par.

اذا كان المسيحي ثابتا في هذا كله هذا الذي تشبه بالمسيح هذا يكون على يمينه يتلو مع الملائكة وينال منه كرامة لانه نال الاكليل الحسن كمل الرتبة وحفظ الامانة وينال الاكليل الذي للحياة الذي بشر به لمحبيه.

اذا اراد المسيحي ان يكون في رتبة ملكية فيبعد عن النساء دفعة واحدة ويرتب في قلبه ان لا يبصرهن ولا يأكل معهن. في العاجل يصرف ذخائره كلها للضعفاء ويدع له حد الملائكة بتواضع القلب والجسم ويكتفي وحده ويكن مثل الطير الذي ليس له آلة ويدفع للمحتاجين من تعب يديه والقرابين والصلاة الكثيرة والصوم الكثير. ويدفع عنه اقاربه بالجسد ويحتمل كل الآلام التي تأتيه من أجل الله ويحمل صليبه ويتبع المخلص ويكن مستعدا للموت في كل وقت لاجل المسيح في الامانة.

لانه لا بد مما يجرب الانسان الذي يطلب الكمال كما جرب سيدنا يسوع المسيح بهذه الثلاث تجارب التي هي الشره والكبرياء ومحبة الذهب.

If a Christian internalizes all of this, he is somebody who resembles Christ, he will be at his right hand, and follow with the angels,[218] and will receive honour from him, because he has obtained the beauteous crown, has completed the course, kept the faith, and[219] received the crown which was promised to those who love him.[220]

If a Christian desires the attainment of an angelic rank he should distance himself from women once and for all,[221] and so fix his heart not to look upon them or to dine with them. Thereupon he should distribute all his goods to the weak and take upon himself the angelic rule in humility of heart and body. He should be self-sufficient, and be like the birds who own nothing.[222] He should give to the needy from the labours[223] of his hands, (with) offerings, frequent prayer, and much fasting. He should put away his family according to the flesh, and should bear all the pains that come to him for the sake of God,[224] and take up his cross and follow the Saviour,[225] being ready for death at all times, on account of Christ and the faith.

Therefore the person who seeks perfection must be tested as our Lord Jesus Christ was tested, by three temptations, and these are greed, pride, and love of money.[226]

---

218 Coquin suggests that the Arabic word here, talā, which usually means to recite, is a mistaken translation of Coptic ⲧⲁⲩⲟ, which may mean "recite" or "send", and thus translates "will be sent with the angels." However, talā can mean "follow", the sense in which it is taken here. In the text I have corrected the plural form yatluwa to the singular yatluw. Coquin had retained the plural in the belief that it reflected a Coptic passive.
219 Coquin deletes this "and".
220 2 Tim 4:7-8; James 1:12.
221 Literally, "on one occasion." A Copticism, rendering ϩⲛ ⲟⲩⲥⲟⲛ.
222 Literally "have no tools." An overliteral translation of Coptic ϩⲛⲁⲁⲩ, a utensil, a tool, or simply a "thing". Cf. Matt 6:26 and par.
223 Literally "tiredness", reflecting κόπος.
224 Cf. Did. 3.10 and par.
225 Cf. Matt 10:38.
226 Almost certainly φιλαργυρία.

ثم ان المجرب جعل همته لمخلصنا وهو صائم وقال له ان كنت انت ابن الله فقل ان تصير هذه الحجارة خبزا. وانت ايضا ايها الناسك تصوم صوما هو لك بسريرتك لا تقبل من افكاره فانه يرضيك ان تخسر عاداتك لا سيما اذا كان صوم دين. بل أجب انت نحو افكارك وتقول مثل سيدك انه ليس يعيش الانسان بالخبز وحده بل بكل كلمة تخرج من فم الله.

هذا الكلام ان تصير هذه الحجارة خبزا له تأويل اخر. لانه يضل محبي الذخائر ان يقال للحجارة تصير ذخائر ويحبون الذخائر حجارة ورملا ويجعلهم يظنون ان يحيوا بها مثل الخبز. ليتذكر كلام الرب القائل ان اذا كثرت ذخائر الواحد فانه لا يجد حياته بهم. ولاجل هذا لا تحبوا فضة يا محبي الله فان أصل الشرور كلها هي محبة الفضة وتكن سريرتك بغير اهتمام. يقول ان لنا طعام وكسوة هذا فلنكتف به. ولكن اسمع كلام الطوباني داود اذ يقول ألق همك للرب وهو يعولك. لا سيما السليح الرسول بطرس يقول ان كل همومكم القوها اليه وهو يقوم بكم.

The tempter then turned his attention to our Saviour while he was fasting and said to him: "If you are the Son of God, tell these stones to become bread." Likewise, ascetic, you fast with a voluntary fast;[227] do not accept his thoughts, for he is persuading you to leave off your observances, especially if should be a fast of religion. Rather give answer to your thoughts,[228] and say, like your master, that a man does not live by bread alone, but by every word which comes out of the mouth of God.

This saying, that that these stones should become bread, has another interpretation. Since those who love material goods are fooled into saying to the stones that they should become material goods; they so love material goods, the stones and the sand, that they are made to think that they can live by them, as it they were bread. The word of the Lord should be remembered, that they will not find life in them if their material goods increase.[229] On this account, you who love God, do not love money, for the root of all evils is the love of money,[230] and let your thoughts be without worry.[231] It is said: "We have food and clothing, let us be satisfied with it."[232] And listen to the word of the blessed David when he says: "Cast your concern onto the Lord as he is supporting you,"[233] and especially the apostle,[234] the apostle Peter says: "Cast all your concerns onto him, as he is concerned for you."[235]

---

227 Literally "a fast according to your will." A Copticism.
228 The word *naḥwa* here is taken by Coquin to mean "in accordance with." Coquin suggests that it would make more sense if the text read "answer your thoughts." I have thus taken *naḥwa* in an adversative sense.
229 Cf. Luke 12:15.
230 1 Tim 6:10.
231 The reading of R, with a negative deleted. m reads: "so that your (plural) life is not without worry." In either event the negative should be deleted.
232 1 Tim 6:8.
233 Ps 55:22 (54:23).
234 Or perhaps "the chief apostle". Two distinct words for apostle are used here.
235 1 Pet 5:7.

فاذا نظر المحتال الى الانسان ان ايمانه هكذا فانه يأتي له التجربة الثانية. لانه أقامه على جناح الهيكل الذي هو كمال الفضائل ويرضي قلبه ان يرفضهم كلهم الذي هو ان ارتم من هذا. ويقول له ان الفضيلة صعبة وانك لا تبق تتصبر هذا التعب لكل الارض. ولم يدعه يتفكر للمخلص القائل لا تهتم لغد. لان كلمن رفع نفسه بالفضيلة من جهة ابليس يقول انه اقبل به الى المدينة المقدسة ولكن لم يدوموا لأنهم لم يقتنوا الفضائل لاجل الله بل لاجل مجد فارغ. الذي هو الحية القائل لكي يكرموا وحدهم من الناس. هؤلاء هكذا يرتمون الى اسفل من جناح الهيكل وينشق من داخلهم ويكون ما داخلهم يخرج ويكونون فراغا اكثر مما كانوا اولا.

بل في الساعة التي يعاهد الانسان عهدا امام الله ويعبده فليتحفظ بكل الثبات لئلا يسقط. مكتوب ان الله لا يهزأ به وانه لا يجرب الله. اذا لم يتيقط الانسان ويبق يذكر الله في كل ساعة فانه يسقط في عبادة الاوثان وهو لا يعلم ما هي عبادة الاوثان الى ان يظن الانسان به وحده انه منتخب وانه خير اكثر من بقية الناس. وهذه هي الكبرياء الطمثة عند الله. اذا ارضى ابليس واحدا انه اخير من الناس كلهم فهذا حقا الذي اسقطه وسجد له لانه لم يعرف كلمة الرب التي قالها اني وديع متواضع بقلبي ولا فهم الكلمة القائلة تسجد للرب الهك وحده وله تعبد. ولاجل هذا يا احبائي اهربوا من عبادة الاوثان التي هي الكبرياء.

When the deceiver[236] sees that such is the fidelity of such a one, so the second temptation comes. For he set him on the pinnacle of the temple, that is to say the perfection of all virtues, and persuades his heart to reject them all: "Throw yourself down from here."[237] He says to him that virtue is hard, "and you will not be able to persevere in this effort for the whole earth." He does not allow him to think of the Saviour who said "Take no thought for tomorrow."[238] Everyone who is lifted up in virtue, it is said, has been brought by the devil to the holy city, but did not last because they did not possess the virtues on account of God but on account of vain glory. That is why[239] the serpent is saying: "They are only honoured by people."[240] These are thus cast down from the pinnacle of the temple and split open from within, and what is within them will come out,[241] and they will be voided yet more than they were beforehand.

However, at the time when a person makes a covenant before God to serve him he should be completely vigilant, so as not to fall. It is written that God is not mocked,[242] and God is not to be tested.[243] If a person is not vigilant, continuing to remember God at every hour, he will fall into the worship of idols, and will not understand that it is the worship of idols until he thinks that he alone is chosen, and better than the rest of the people.[244] And this is pride, impure before God. If the devil persuades the person that he is superior to other people, so he will indeed be falling down and worshipping him, because he did not know the word of the Lord which says: "I am meek, and humble in my heart",[245] and he has not understood the word which says: "You shall bow down to the Lord, and serve him alone."[246] On this account, beloved, flee the service of idols; and this is pride.

---

236 I have conjectured *almuḥtālu* instead of the *almuḥālu* of the MSS.
237 Matt 4:6.
238 Matt 6:34.
239 Literally, "that is to say." Coquin suggests that ⲉⲧⲉ ⲡⲁⲓ and ⲉⲧⲃⲉ ⲡⲁⲓ have been confused.
240 Matt 6:2.
241 Acts 1:18.
242 Gal 6:7. This citation is omitted by m.
243 Deut 6:16; Matt 4:7.
244 Coquin picks up an allusion to Wis 14:14, which states that idolatry entered the world through vainglory.
245 Matt 11:29.
246 Matt 4;10. The MSS read "You shall bow down to the Lord alone, and serve (imperative) him" due to confusion in the rendering of the Coptic; the Arabic rendering of the second verb, as Coquin observes, is a misreading of a Coptic conjunctive. The Arabic text has been corrected, at the suggestion of Rifaat Ebied.

ونحب بعضنا بعضا ونكن محبين للغرباء ومحبين للتعليم ونهرب من كل شريك سوء ونسرع المضي الى عبيد الله ونتعبد معهم لان ارراكا قالت لداود هذه عبدتك مستعدة تكون لك عبدة اغسل ارجل عبيدك لكي نغسل نحن ايضا ارجل القديسين. لنسمع ممن هو اعظم من داود يسوع المسيح ربنا ان مثالكم المبارك. لانه يجيب لكل واحد ممن حفظ وصاياه جيدا ايها العبد الخير الامين صرت امينا على القليل اني اجعلك على كثير ادخل الى فرح سيدك.

نكون بحق ان يقول لكل واحد منا المجتمعين باسمه. تعالوا يا مبركي أني رثوا الملك المعد لكم من قبل انشاء العالم. جعت فاطعمتموني وعطشت فسقيتموني وكنت غريبا فآويتموني وكنت عريانا فكسوتموني وكنت مريضا فعدتموني وكنت مسجونا فتفقدتموني. قال فانهم يجيبون الابرار ويقولون له يا رب متى رأيناك جائعا فطعمناك والاخر الاتية بعد هذا فعلناه بك؟ فيجيب ويقول الحق اقول لكم انما فعلتموه مع هؤلاء الاخوة الصغار فانا الذي فعلتموه بي.

Let us love one another,[247] let us be hospitable,[248] loving instruction,[249] let us flee from any wicked companion and hasten towards the servants of God and serve them,[250] since Abigail said to David, "Here is your servant, ready to be your servant, washing the feet of your servants"[251] so that we ourselves should wash the feet of the saints.[252] Let us listen to one greater than David, Jesus Christ Our Lord, your blessed example.[253] For to each of those who kept his commandments well he said: "Well done, good and faithful servant. Since you have been faithful in a little, I am putting you in charge of a great deal. Enter into the joy of your Lord."[254]

It is in truth[255] that he will say to all of you gathered in his name: "Come, blessed of my Father, inherit the Kingdom prepared for you since the beginning of the world. I hungered and so you fed me, and I was thirsty and so you gave me a drink, and I was a stranger and so you lodged me, and I was naked and so you clothed me, and I was sick and so you visited me, and I was a prisoner and you attended to me." So he said, and then the righteous answered him saying: "Lord, when did we see you hungry and so fed you, and the other things after that, and we did them for you?" He answered and said to them: "In truth I say to you, as you did it for one of these little brothers,[256] so it was for me that you did it."[257]

---

247 1 John 4:7.
248 Literally "loving to strangers", representing φιλόξενοι.
249 φιλομαθής.
250 The MSS have "serve with them." Coquin suggests a confusion between ⲙ̄ⲙⲟⲩ (an oblique object of the verb) and ⲛ̄ⲙⲙⲁⲩ (with them).
251 1 Sam 25:41.
252 1 Tim 5:10.
253 For "your blessed example". m reads "dwellings for the angels". The difference is relatively slight in Arabic so a simple textual corruption is readily explicable.
254 Matt 25:21.
255 Literally "We are in truth..." A paraphrastic Coptic expression, preserved in R though corrected in m.
256 "As... brothers" so R. m reads: "each time that you did it for one of these little ones..."
257 Matt 25:34–40.

ومن يحفظ هذه القوانين سلام الرب عليه والرحمة وعلى كل اسرائيل الله. والعدو لا يريح فيهم بل يستريحون مع كل الاطهار في ملكوت سيدنا يسوع المسيح هذا من جهته المجد للاب والروح القدس الى ابد الابدين. آمين.


كملت قوانين القديس ابوليدس اول اساقفة رومية التي للرسل بسلام الرب له الشكر والمجد دائما ابدا.

May the peace of the Lord, and mercy, be on anyone who keeps these canons, and the whole Israel of God:[258] may the enemy not find rest in them, but may they find rest with the all the pure in the Kingdom of our Lord Jesus Christ, through whom may glory be to the Father and to the Holy Spirit into the ages of the ages. Amen.

*A translator's postscript:*
The conclusion of the canons of Saint Hippolytus, the archbishop of Rome, the apostolic,[259] in the peace of the Lord, to whom be the praise and the glory, always, for ever.[260]

---

258 Cf. Gal 6:16.
259 This term might also apply to the canons themselves, rather than Hippolytus.
260 So R. m reads: The conclusion of the canons of Saint Hippolytus, the archbishop of Rome, which he composed. May God help us to keep them. Their number is thirty-eight. To God be the glory always, for ever, into eternity.

# Bibliography

**On the *Canones Hippolyti*:**

Achelis, Hans    *Die ältesten Quellen des orientalischen Kirchenrechts 1: die Canones Hippolyti* (TU 6.4; Leipzig: Hinrichs, 1891).

Arendzen, J.P.    "The XXXII Canon of Hippolytus", *JTS* 4 (1903), 282–85.

Barrett-Lennard, Ric    "The Canons of Hippolytus and Christian concern with illness, health, and healing", *JECS* 13 (2005), 137–164.

Baumstark, Anton    "Kanones des Hippolytos oder Kanones des Iulius", *OrChr* 2 (1902), 191–196.

Botte, B.    "L'origine des Canons d'Hippolyte", in *Mélanges en l'honneur de Monseigneur Michel Andrieu* (Strasbourg: Palais Universitaire, 1956), 53–63.

Bradshaw, Paul F. (ed.) (Carol Bebawi trans.), *The Canons of Hippolytus* (Bramcote: Grove, 1987).

Brakmann, Heinzgard    "Alexandreia und die Kanones des Hippolyt", *JAC* 22 (1979), 139–149.

Burkitt, F. C.    "The baptismal rite in the *Canons of Hippolytus*", *JTS* 1 (1900), 279.

Coquin, René-Georges    *Les canons d'Hippolyte: Édition critique de la version arabe, introduction et traduction française* (Patrologia Orientalis 31.2; Paris: Firmin-Didot 1966).

Haneberg, D.B. von    *Canones S Hippolyti Arabice e codicibus Romanis cum versione latina, annotationibus et prolegomenis* (Munich: Academia Boica, 1870).

Hanssens, Jean Michel    "L'édition critique des Canons d'Hippolyte", *OCP* 32 (1966), 536–544.

Jourdan, G.V.    "'Agape' or 'Lord's supper': a study of certain passages in the *Canons of Hippolytus*", *Hermathena* 64 (1944), 32–43.

Malvy, Antoine    "L'onction des malades dans les Canons d'Hippolyte et les documents apparentés", *RSR* 9 (1919), 222–229.

Morin, G.    "L'origine des Canons d'Hippolyte", *RBén* 17 (1900), 241–46.

Müller, Karl    "Kleine Beiträge zur alten Kirchengeschichte 6", *ZNW* 23 (1924), 226–31.

Riedel, Wilhelm "Bemerkungen zu den Kanones des Hippolytus", *TSK* 76 (1903), 338–342.

Riedel, Wilhelm *Die Kirchenrechtsquellen des Patriarchats Alexandrien* (Leipzig: Deichert, 1900).

**Other literature cited (which may include mention of *Canones Hippolyti*)**

Aubineau, Michel "Les écrits de saint Athanase sur la virginité", *Revue d'ascétique et de mystique* 31 (1955), 140–173.

Batiffol, Pierre *Études d'histoire et de théologie positive [1er série]: la discipline de l'arcane; les origines de la pénitence; la hierarchie primitive; l'agape* (3rd ed.; Paris: Lecoffre, 1904).

Beveridge, William *ΣΥΝΟΔΙΚΟΝ, sive pandectae canonum SS. apostolorum et conciliorum ab ecclesia Graeca receptorum, nec non canonicarum SS patrum epistolarum* (Oxford: Sheldonian Theatre, 1672).

Bradshaw, Paul F. *Rites of ordination: their history and theology* (London: SPCK, 2014).

Bradshaw, Paul F. "'Diem baptismo sollemniorem': initiation and Easter in Christian antiquity", in Maxwell E. Johnson (ed.), *Living water, sealing Spirit: readings in Christian initiation* (Collegeville: Liturgical,1995), 137–47.

Bradshaw, Paul F. *Daily prayer in the early church* (London: SPCK, 1981).

Brightman, F.E. *Liturgies eastern and western* (Oxford, Clarendon, 1896).

Buchinger, Harald "Breaking the fast: the central moment of the Paschal celebration in historical context and diachronic perspective", in Paul van Geest et al. (eds.), *Sanctifying texts, transforming rituals: encounters in liturgical studies* (Leiden: Brill, 2017), 192–205.

Buchinger, Harald "The Easter cycle in late antique Cappadocia: revisiting some well-known witnesses", *Bollettino della Badia Greca di Grottaferrata* (3rd series) 11 (2014), 45–77.

Buonopane, Alfredo "Medicae nell'occidente romano: un'indagine preliminare", in Alfredo Buonopane, Francesca Cenerini, *Donna e lavoro nella documentazione epigrafica* (Faenza: Fratelli Lega, 2003), 113–130.

Camplani, Alberto and Federico Contardi "Remarks on the textual contribution of the Coptic codices preserving the Canons of Saint Basil with edition of the ordination rite for the bishop (canon 16)", in Francesca P. Barone et al. (eds.), *Philologie, herméneutique et histoire des textes entre orient et occident: mélanges en hommage à Sever J. Voicu* (Turnhout: Brepols, 2017), 139–159.

Chase, Nathan — "Another look at the 'daily office' in the Apostolic Tradition", *Studia liturgica* 49 (2019), 5–25.

Cirlot, Felix — *The early Eucharist* (London: SPCK, 1939).

Connolly, R.H. — *The So-called Egyptian Church Order and derived documents* (Cambridge: Cambridge University Press, 1916).

Crislip, Andrew T. — *From monastery to hospital: Christian monasticism and the transformation of health care in late antiquity* (Ann Arbor: University of Michigan, 2005).

Crum, W.E. (ed.) — *Der Papyruscodex saec. VI-VII der Phillippsbibliothek in Cheltenham: koptische theologische Schriften* (Strassburg: Trübner, 1915).

Cuming, G.J. — "Egyptian elements in the Jerusalem liturgy", *JTS* (ns) 25 (1974), 117–124.

DiLuzio, Meghan J. — *A place at the altar: priestesses in republican Rome* (Princeton: Princeton University Press, 2016).

Frank, P. Suso — *ΑΓΓΕΛΙΚΟΣ ΒΙΟΣ: begriffsanalytische und begriffsgeschichtliche Untersuchung zum "engelgleichen Leben", im frühen Mönchtum* (Münster: Aschendorff, 1964).

Hamman, A. — *Vie liturgique et vie sociale: repas des pauvres, diaconie et diaconat, agapē et repas de charité, offrande dans l'antiquité chrétienne* (Paris: Desclée, 1968).

Horden, Peregrine — "Poverty, charity, and the invention of the hospital", in Scott Fitzgerald Johnson (ed.) *The Oxford Handbook of Late Antiquity* (Oxford: Oxford University Press, 2012), 715–743.

Jasper, R.C.D., G.J. Cuming (eds.) — *Prayers of the Eucharist: early and reformed* (3rd ed.; Collegeville: Liturgical, 1987).

Johnson, Maxwell E. *St Cyril of Jerusalem: lectures on the Christian sacraments* (Yonkers: St Vladimir's Seminary Press, 2017).

Klauck, Hans-Josef — *The apocryphal acts of the the apostles: an introduction* (ETr; Waco TX: Baylor University Press, 2008).

Kretschmar, Georg — "Beiträge zur Geschichte der Liturgie, inbesondere der Taufliturgie, in Ägypten", *Jahrbuch für Liturgik und Hymnologie* 8 (1963), 1–54.

Lanne, E. "La confession de foi baptismale à Alexandrie et à Rome", in A.M. Triacca and A. Pistoia (eds.), *La liturgie: expression de la foi* (Rome: CLV, 1979), 213–228.

Leutholf, Hiob (Ludolfus) *Iobi Ludolfi alias Leutholf dicti ad suam Historiam Aethiopicam antehac commentarius* (Frankfurt am M: Zunner, 1691).

Lietzmann, Hans *Messe und Herrenmahl: eine Studie zur Geschichte der Liturgie* (Bonn: Marcus und Weber, 1926).

Lim, Richard *Public disputation, power, and social order in late antiquity* (Berkeley: University of California Press, 1995).

Lollar, Jacob A., *The history of John the son of Zebedee* (Piscataway NJ: Gorgias, 2020).

Maclean, A.J. *The ancient church orders* (Cambridge: Cambridge University Press, 1910).

Markschies, Christoph "Wer schrieb die sogenannte *Traditio apostolica*? Neue Beobachtungen und Hypothesen zu einer kaum lösbaren Frage aus der altkirchlichen Literaturegeschichte", in Wolfram Kinzig, Christoph Markschies, Markus Vinzent (eds.), *Tauffragen und Bekenntnis* (Berlin: de Gruyter, 1999), 1–74.

Miller, Timothy S. *The birth of the hospital in the Byzantine Empire* (Baltimore: Johns Hopkins University Press, 1985).

Pitra, J.B. *Iuris ecclesiastici Graecorum historia et monumenta* (Rome: Collegium Urbanum, 1864).

Psarev, Andrei V. "The 19th Canonical Answer of Timothy of Alexandria: on the history of sacramental oikonomia", *SVTQ* 51 (2007), 297–320.

Reicke, Bo *Diakonie, Festfreude und Zelos: in Verbindung mit der altchristlichen Agapefeier* (Uppsala: Lundequist, 1951).

Reynolds, Philip Lyndon *Marriage in the western church* (Leiden: Brill, 2001).

Rouwhorst, G.A.M. *Les hymnes pascales d'Ephrem de Nisibe* I (Leiden: Brill, 1989).

Schwartz, E. Über die pseudapostolischen Kirchenordnungen (Schriften der wissenschaftlichen Gesellschaft im Strassburg 6; Strassburg: Trübner, 1910).

Stewart(-Sykes), Alistair *Hippolytus: on the apostolic tradition* (Yonkers NY: St Vladimir's Seminary Press, 2015).

Stewart(-Sykes), Alistair    *The Gnomai of the Council of Nicaea: the Coptic text, with English translation and introduction* (Piscataway NJ: Gorgias, 2015).

Stewart(-Sykes), Alistair    "The early Alexandrian baptismal creed: declaratory, interrogatory... or both?", *Questions liturgiques* 95 (2014), 237–253.

Stewart(-Sykes), Alistair    *The original bishops* (Grand Rapids: Baker Academic, 2014).

Stewart(-Sykes), Alistair    *On the two ways* (Yonkers NY: St Vladimir's Seminary Press, 2011).

Stewart(-Sykes), Alistair    "Milch", in Georg Schöllgen et al. (eds.), *Reallexikon für Antike und Christentum* 24 (Stuttgart: Anton Hiersmann, 2011), 784–803.

Stewart(-Sykes), Alistair    *Two early Egyptian liturgical papyri: the Deir Balyzeh papyrus and the Barcelona papyrus with appendices containing comparative material* (JLS 70; Norwich: Hymns ancient and modern, 2010).

Stewart(-Sykes), Alistair    *The Didascalia apostolorum: an English version* (Turnhout: Brepols, 2009).

Stewart(-Sykes), Alistair    *The Lamb's high feast: Melito, Peri Pascha, and the Quartodeciman Paschal liturgy at Sardis* (Leiden: Brill, 1998).

Strobel, August    *Ursprung und Geschichte des frühchristlichen Osterkalenders* (Berlin: Akademie, 1977).

Till, Walter and Johannes Leipoldt    *Der koptische Text der Kirchenordnung Hippolyts* (Berlin: Akademie, 1954).

Vansleb, J.M.    *Histoire de l'église d'Alexandrie* (Paris: Chez la veuve Clousier, 1677).

Wendebourg, Dorothea    "Die altestamentlichen Reinheitsgesetze in der frühen Kirche", *ZKG* 95 (1984), 149–170.

Whitaker, E. C.    "The history of the baptismal formula", *JEH* 16 (1965), 1–12.

Wilken, Robert L.    *John Chrysostom and the Jews: rhetoric and reality in the late fourth century* (Berkeley: University of California Press, 1983).

Yarnold, E.J.    *The awe-inspiring rites of initiation* (2nd ed.; Collegeville: Liturgical, 1994).

# Indices

**Index locorum:**
**1. Scripture**

| | |
|---|---|
| Gen 8:21 | 77 |
| Exod 12:7 | 133 |
| 28:35 | 133 |
| Lev 12.1-5 | 107 |
| Deut 6:16 | 163 |
| 25:13 | 157 |
| 1 Sam 25:41 | 165 |
| Ps 51:14 (50:12) | 75 |
| 55:22 (54:23) | 161 |
| 65:11 (64:12) | 36, 145 |
| 77:6 (76:7) | 125 |
| 96:5 (95:5) | 95 |
| 119:62 (118:62) | 125 |
| 132:4-5 (131:4-5) | 149 |
| Prov 20:10, 23 | 157 |
| 26:11 | 151 |
| Wis 14:14 | 163 |
| Sir 24:15 | 129 |
| 39:13-14 | 129 |
| 41:21 | 157 |
| Isa 11:19 | 123 |
| Matt 4:6 | 163 |
| 4:7 | 163 |
| 4:10 | 163 |
| 5:13 | 143 |
| 6:2 | 163 |
| 6:26 | 159 |
| 6:34 | 163 |
| 10:38 | 159 |
| 11:29 | 163 |
| 16:27 | 149 |
| 25:6 | 129 |
| 25:34-40 | 165 |
| 25:21 | 165 |
| 25:41 | 153 |
| Mark 13:35 | 129 |
| Luke 9:51 | 141 |
| 12:15 | 161 |
| John 5:29 | 149 |
| 12:26 | 81 |
| Acts 1:18 | 163 |
| 1:24 | 77 |
| 5:15 | 123 |
| 6:8 | 81 |
| 16:25 | 125 |
| Rom 8:17 | 121 |
| 12:11 | 151 |
| 16:20 | 77 |
| 1 Cor 3:11 | 121 |
| 14:34 | 89 |
| 2 Cor. 1:22 | 113 |
| Gal 6:7 | 163 |
| 6:16 | 167 |
| Eph 5:18 | 155 |
| Phil 3:10-11 | 121 |
| Col 1:16 | 73 |
| 1:23 | 157 |
| 1 Tim 2:9-12 | 103 |
| 3:2 | 75, 155 |
| 3:3 | 155 |
| 3:8 | 155 |
| 4:13 | 119 |
| 5:3 | 89 |
| 5:3-15 | 89 |
| 5:10 | 165 |
| 5:17 | 89 |
| 6:8 | 161 |
| 6:10 | 161 |
| 2 Tim 2:12 | 121 |

|  |  |  |  |  |  |
|---|---|---|---|---|---|
|  | 4:7-8 | 159 |  | 4:13 | 121 |
| Titus | 1:6-7 | 75, 155 |  | 5:7 | 161 |
|  | 1:16 | 151 | 2 Pet | 2:22 | 151 |
| James | 1:12 | 159 | 1 John | 4:7 | 165 |
| 1 Pet | 3:3 | 103 | Rev | 2:17 | 12, 135 |

## 2. Ancient Christian literature

### 2.1 Anonymous church order literature (excluding *Canones Hippolyti* and *Traditio apostolica*)

*Apostolic church order*

| | |
|---|---|
| 11 | 24 |
| 12 | 25 |
| 13.2 | 127 |
| 16 | 46 |
| 21 | 89 |
| 21.2. | 155 |

*Can. Athan.*

| | |
|---|---|
| 28 | 18 |
| 49 | 60 |

*Can. Bas.*

| | |
|---|---|
| 96 | 18, 32, 131 |

*Const. ap.*

| | |
|---|---|
| 3.16 | 55 |
| 6.30.2 | 141 |
| 7.44 | 129 |
| 8.4 | 23 |
| 8.5 | 38 |
| 8.12 | 133 |
| 8.18 | 42, 47 |
| 8.26.1-3 | 87 |
| 8.29 | 61 |

*Didasc. ap.*

| | |
|---|---|
| 2.28.1 | 59, 145 |
| 5.5.4-6 | 24, 25 |
| 5.18b-5.19.1 | 24, 26 |
| 6.22.2 | 141 |

*Fides patrum*

| | |
|---|---|
| 1 | 33 |

*Sent. Conc. Nic.*

| | |
|---|---|
| 1.11-12 | 153 |
| 2.1-4 | 44 |
| 3.2 | 105 |
| 4.3 | 30, 103 |
| 4.5 | 30, 103 |
| 6.5 | 28, 30 |
| 7.1 | 31, 101 |
| 8.14 | 31, 119 |
| 15.7 | 31 |

*Test. Dom.*

| | |
|---|---|
| 1.19 | 41, 57, 133 |
| 1.22 | 44, 131 |
| 1.23 | 43, 57, 133 |
| 1.32 | 44 |
| 1.42 | 44 |
| 2.9 | 115 |
| 2.11 | 137 |
| 2.19 | 44, 56 |
| 2.24 | 44, 125 |

*Did.*

| | |
|---|---|
| 2.2 | 21, 155 |
| 2.3 | 21, 155 |
| 2.6 | 21, 155 |
| 3.2 | 21, 155 |
| 3.3 | 21, 155 |
| 3.5 | 155 |
| 3.6 | 21, 155 |
| 3.7 | 155 |

| | | |
|---|---|---|
| 3.8 | 21, 155 | |
| 3.9 | 155 | |
| 3.10 | 155, 159 | |
| 4.1 | 25, 127 | |
| 4.5 | 157 | |
| 4.8 | 157 | |
| 4.9 | 155 | |
| 4.13 | 157 | |
| 14.1 | 75 | |

## 2.2 Conciliar canons
Constantinople
    7 (spurious)     54
Nicaea
    16     89
    18     15, 135
Laodicea
    28     139

## 2.3 Other early Christian literature
Anon. *Chronicon Paschale*
    350     39
    360     40
– *Hist. Johannis* (Syriac)
    22     48
    30     48
– *Odes Sol.*
    11.15     129
– *Vit. Pol.*
    22     38, 42, 75
ps-Athanasius *Virg.*
    7     27, 30
    8     27
    20     44
    22     27
*Barn.*
    19.5a     127
Basil *Ep.*
    93     131
    94     150
    125     4
    150     40
    159.2     49
    188.13     47
– *De Sancto Spirito*
    10.24     49
    12.28     49
– *Reg. Fus.*
    37     44, 125
ps-Cyril of Alexandria *Erotapokrisis Cyrilli et Stephani*
         50
Cyril of Jerusalem *Cat. myst.*
    1.9     48
    3.4     54
ps-Clement *Ad Jac.*
    5     38
– *Hom.*
    3.60-72     38
    11.1     149
    11.28     149
Dionysius Alex. *Ad Basileiden*
    1     117
    2     22
Epiphanius *Pan.*
    75.3.7     40
Eusebius *Hist. Eccl.*
    7.22.1-11     39
Evagrius *De malignis cogitationibus*
    1     29
– *Or.*
    40     30
    113     29
    142     30
– *Sent. ad Virg.*
    4     28
Gelasius Cyzicus *Syntagma*
    2.23.5     52
Gregory of Nazianzus *Or.*
    43.63     40
– *Somnium de anastasiae ecclesia*

| | | | |
|---|---|---|---|
| 11-13 | 18, 42 | Socrates *Hist. Eccl.* | |
| John Cassian *Conf.* | | 5.22 | 75, 131 |
| 5 | 29 | Sozomen *Hist. Eccl.* | |
| – *Inst.* | | 3.16.12-16 | 40 |
| 2.5 | 44 | 4.20.2 | 39 |
| 3.5 | 44 | 6.34 | 40 |
| John Chrysostom *Ad Stagirium* | | Synesius *Ep.* | |
| 3.13 | 39 | 67 | 38 |
| – *Hom. in Matt.* | | Timothy of Alexandria *Resp. can.* | |
| 54.7 | 47 | 6 | 22 |
| – *Hom. 33 in Hebr.* | | 38 (spurious) | 50 |
| 13.4 | 39 | Theodore of Mopsuestia *Cat. Myst.* | |
| Leo I *Ep.* | | 14.27 | 55 |
| 167, *inquisitio* 4 | 161 | Theodoret *Hist. Eccl.* | |
| Liberatus *Brev.* | 38 | 1.4 | 52 |
| Sarapion *Sacr.* | | 5.18.2-5 | 39 |
| 5 | 61 | Theophanis *Chronographia* | |
| 11 | 55 | 5824 | 39 |
| 17 | 61 | | |

## 3. Other ancient sources

### 3.1 Literary sources

Catullus *Carm.*
    61.8-10    103
    68.133    103
Julian *Ep.*
    22    40
Lucan *Pharsalia*
    2.360-364    103
Pliny *Nat. Hist.*
    21.46    103
Soranus *Gyn.*
    1.3-4    107
Ulpian *apud Digesta*
    1.18.6.8    99

### 3.2 Non-literary sources

P.Mich. 434    103
P.Mil.Vogl. 85    103
P.Oxy. 267    103
P.Oxy. 795    103
P.Oxy. 905    103
SIG 888.39-44    141

## Index nominum:

Achelis, Hans, 1, 2, 3, 6, 19, 20, 34, 42, 59, 75, 85, 101, 113, 137,
Arendzen, J.P., 139
Aubineau, Michel, 28
Barrett-Lennard, Ric, 7, 40, 60, 61, 87, 123
Baumstark, Anton, 1
Bebawi, Carol, 99, 103, 129, 133, 143
Beveridge, William, 54
Botte, B., 3, 5, 6, 52, 53, 65
Bradshaw, Paul F., 2, 9, 11, 12, 13, 23, 33, 42, 43, 44, 47, 54, 55, 77, 87, 89, 99, 103, 109, 113, 125, 129, 131, 133, 139, 143, 149,
Brakmann, Heinzgard, 36, 37, 38, 51
Brightman, F.E., 77
Buchinger, Harald, 56
Burkitt, F. C., 111
Buonopane, Alfredo, 107
Camplani, Alberto, 32
Chase, Nathan, 44
Cirlot, Felix, 139
Connolly, R.H., 2, 3, 7, 13, 14, 15, 19, 20, 24, 35, 36,
Contardi, Federico, 32
Coquin, René-Georges, 2, 3, 4, 5, 6, 12, 22, 24, 25, 26, 27, 28, 29, 30, 31, 34, 35, 37, 43, 52, 58, 62, 65, 71, 75, 77, 79, 81, 83, 85, 89, 91, 93, 95, 97, 99, 103, 105, 107, 109, 111, 113, 115, 117, 121,123, 135, 127, 129, 133, 135, 139, 141, 143, 145, 149, 151, 155, 157, 159, 161, 163, 165
Crislip, Andrew T., 40-41
Crum, W.E., 50
Cuming, G.J., 35, 54, 145
DiLuzio, Meghan J., 103
Frank, P. Suso, 30
Hamman, A., 59
Haneberg, D.B. von, 1, 20, 58, 103, 105, 129, 133, 139, 141, 151
Hanssens, Jean Michel, 22, 27, 35, 38, 49, 65, 115
Horden, Peregrine, 39, 40, 41
Jasper, R.C.D., 35
Johnson, Maxwell E., 54
Jourdan, G.V., 139
Kretschmar, Georg, 34, 51
Klauck, Hans-Josef, 49
Lanne, E., 52
Leutholf, Hiob (Ludolfus), 1
Lietzmann, Hans, 59, 139
Lim, Richard, 52
Lollar, Jacob A., 48
Malvy, Antoine, 119
Markschies, Christoph, 5
Maclean, A.J., 2, 6
Miller, Timothy S., 39
Morin, G., 34
Müller, Karl, 46
Pitra, J.B., 50
Psarev, A.V., 90
Reicke, Bo, 141
Reynolds, Philip Lyndon, 101
Riedel, Wilhelm, 1, 2, 27, 28, 30, 46, 53, 58, 62, 65, 83, 105, 113, 121, 129, 131, 135, 139, 151
Rouwhorst, G.A.M., 26
Schwartz, E., 2, 3
Stewart(-Sykes), Alistair, 10, 21, 25, 26, 31, 36, 46, 47, 51, 58, 62, 65, 83, 105, 113, 121, 129, 131, 135, 139, 151
Strobel, August, 56
Till, Walter, 51
Vansleb, J.M., 1
Wendebourg, Dorothea, 43
Whitaker, E. C., 49, 50
Wilken, Robert L., 43
Yarnold, E.J., 55

www.ingramcontent.com/pod-product-compliance
Lightning Source LLC
Chambersburg PA
CBHW071733080526
44588CB00013B/2006